# JONAH

## a whale of a lesson on obedience

## John Goetsch

First published in 2007 by Striving Together Publications, a ministry of Lancaster Baptist Church, Lancaster, CA 93535. Striving Together Publications is committed to providing tried, trusted, and proven books that will further equip local churches to carry out the Great Commission. Your comments and suggestions are valued.

Striving Together Publications
4020 E. Lancaster Blvd.
Lancaster, CA 93535
800.201.7748

Cover design by Jeremy Lofgren
Layout by Craig Parker
Edited by Danielle Mordh
Special thanks to our proofreaders.

ISBN 978-1-59894-029-9

**Printed in the United States of America**

# Table of Contents

# How to Use This Curriculum

Take a moment to familiarize yourself with the features of this *Striving Together* Sunday school curriculum:

## Schedule

The lessons contained in this curriculum are undated, allowing you to begin and end the teaching series at any time. There are thirteen lessons that traditionally may be taught weekly any time of the year.

## Student Edition Books

Companion books are available through *Striving Together Publications*. These contain:

- The outlines with blanks that students may fill in during the lessons

- Various Scripture quotations that are used throughout each lesson
- The introductory lesson overviews
- Study questions for review throughout the week
- A suggested memory verse for each lesson

These books are excellent tools for the members of a class. We suggest ordering enough books for each member of the class, plus additional copies for new members who enroll in the class throughout the teaching series. Giving class members a study book encourages faithfulness to the class, provides students with a devotional tool for use throughout the week, and allows them to review what they learned previously.

## Key Verses

The verses from which the lessons are taken are included at the beginning of each lesson. These are provided so that you may read them through several times in prayerful preparation for your time in class. Many teachers choose to memorize their key verses. During the class hour, we suggest that you use your own Bible for Scripture reading and encourage your class members to do so as well.

## Overview and Theme

The overview and theme sections are provided so that you may be aware of the overall emphasis of each lesson, especially as they relate to the other lessons in the curriculum. These brief statements provide a snapshot of where each lesson will take the students.

## Lesson Objectives

Bible teaching has a higher goal than the delivery of information. That goal is a life-change. Students want to know what they are to do with what they are given from God's Word. As you prepare for and teach each lesson, emphasize how those listening may apply its truths throughout the week.

## Teaching Outline

The abbreviated outline enables you to view the entire lesson at a glance to see how the content fits together. Teaching with an organized outline increases the students' abilities to understand and remember the lesson content.

# Overview of the Book of Jonah

## Key Verses

*"Now the word of the LORD came unto Jonah the son of Amittai, saying, Arise, go to Nineveh, that great city, and cry against it; for their wickedness is come up before me. But Jonah rose up to flee unto Tarshish from the presence of the LORD, and went down to Joppa; and he found a ship going to Tarshish: so he paid the fare thereof, and went down into it, to go with them unto Tarshish from the presence of the LORD."*—JONAH 1:1–3

## Overview

When God speaks, it is absolutely essential that we listen. Many voices cry out to us today in an attempt to pull us away from the will of God. Failure to hear and obey God's voice spells disaster every time. The old hymn writer, John H. Sammis, had it right: "When we walk with the Lord in the light of His Word, what a glory He sheds on our way! While we do His good will He abides with us still, and with all who will trust and obey. Trust and obey, for there's no other way, to be happy in Jesus, but to trust and obey."

## Lesson Theme

Obedience brings God's blessing in our lives while disobedience to the will of God results in disaster.

# Lesson Objectives

- To help the student understand that God has a plan for every person's life.
- To enable the student to identify the personal rebellion that is a part of our sinful human nature.
- To cause the student to realize that our disobedience has a negative ramification on others, as well as on ourselves.
- To encourage the student to make decisions that will form a pattern of obedience to the will of God.

# Teaching Outline

I. Jonah's Name
    A. The Son of Truth
    B. The Solution to Turmoil

II. Jonah's Negligence
    A. A Willful Deafness
    B. A Woeful Disaster

III. Jonah's Nation
    A. The Nemesis of Indifference
    B. The Necessity of Involvement

IV. Jonah's Notoriety
    A. A Legacy of Disobedience
    B. A Lesson in Decisions

# Overview of the Book of Jonah

## Text

*"Now the word of the LORD came unto Jonah the son of Amittai, saying, Arise, go to Nineveh, that great city, and cry against it; for their wickedness is come up before me. But Jonah rose up to flee unto Tarshish from the presence of the LORD, and went down to Joppa; and he found a ship going to Tarshish: so he paid the fare thereof, and went down into it, to go with them unto Tarshish from the presence of the LORD."*—JONAH 1:1–3

Most of us have heard the story of "Jonah and the Whale" since we were little children. It is certainly one of those "attention-getting" stories in the Old Testament. Many skeptics of the Bible use this story to support their arguments against the inerrancy of the Scriptures. Jesus Himself, however, prophetically pointed to this story as an accurate fact of history when He stated in Matthew 12:40, *"For as Jonas was three days and three nights in the whale's belly; so shall the Son of man be three days and three nights in the heart of the earth."*

What does this story teach us in our lives today? Sure, it's a fun story to dramatize. We all chuckle at the dilemma of Jonah in the belly of a fish, but what does that have to do with living for God in the twenty-first century? Is it really important to do *exactly* what God says *every* time He speaks? Does God really know what is best? If we do obey God, will it make a difference in our society?

The book of Jonah teaches us what the writer John reiterated eight times in the book of Revelation: *"He that hath an ear, let him hear what the Spirit saith...."*

# I.  Jonah's Name

Our names are important when we receive them at birth, but it is essential that we build good reputations with the names we have received. Proverbs 22:1 says, *"A good name is rather to be chosen than great riches, and loving favour rather than silver and gold."* Solomon says, *"A good name is better than precious ointment..."* (Ecclesiastes 7:1).

Certain names, such as the Apostle Paul, bring with them great reputations of honor and credibility, while others, such as Adolph Hitler bring with them shame and reproach. Proverbs 10:7 states it well, *"The memory of the just is blessed: but the name of the wicked shall rot."*

## A.  The Son of Truth

The name, Amittai, (Jonah's father), means "truth." Therefore, Jonah was literally the "son of truth." Unfortunately, as we shall see from this series of lessons, Jonah was not very faithful with the truth he received.

In John 14:6, Jesus declared, *"…I am the way, the* **truth***, and the life.…"* In John 8:32, Jesus tells us, *"And ye shall know the* **truth***, and the* **truth** *shall make you free."*

Every child of God is, in reality, a "son of truth." God has given us His Word, and He demands that we be faithful with it in our lives.

*"I have given them thy word; and the world hath hated them, because they are not of the world, even as I am not of the world. I pray not that thou shouldest take them out of the world, but that thou shouldest keep them from the evil. They are not of the world, even as I am not of the world. Sanctify them through thy truth: thy word is truth. As thou hast sent me into the world, even so have I also sent them into the world."*—JOHN 17:14–18

## B. The Solution to Turmoil

There never has been, nor will there ever be, a problem that the preaching of God's Word cannot solve.

*"For as the rain cometh down, and the snow from heaven, and returneth not thither, but watereth the earth, and maketh it bring forth and bud, that it may give seed to the sower, and bread to the eater: So shall my word be that goeth forth out of my mouth: it shall not return unto me void, but it shall accomplish that which I please, and it shall prosper in the thing whereto I sent it."*—ISAIAH 55:10–11

Man often is unaware of his condition or his need. Jeremiah 17:9 states, *"The heart is deceitful above all things, and desperately wicked: who can know it?"* But, Hebrews 4:12 declares, *"…the word of God is quick, and powerful, and sharper than any twoedged sword, piercing even to the dividing asunder of soul and spirit, and of the joints and marrow, and is a discerner of the thoughts and intents of the heart."*

God uses the preaching of His Word to change lives. *"But hath in due times manifested his word through preaching…"* (Titus 1:3). Yes, it pleases God, *"…by the foolishness of preaching to save them that believe"* (1 Corinthians 1:21).

# II. Jonah's Negligence

Jonah was not very faithful to the truth he had received. Emerson once stated, "The greatest homage we can pay to truth is to use it." John Locke declared, "Error is none the better for being common, nor truth the worse for having lain neglected." Paul wisely admonished us in 2 Corinthians 13:8, *"For we can do nothing **against** the truth, but **for** the truth"* (emphasis mine).

## A. *A Willful Deafness*

When God said, **"Go"**—Jonah said **"No."**

Sadly, we often know exactly what God is saying. We know exactly what He wants us to do, but we willfully turn a deaf ear! Second Peter 3:5 speaks of this negligence with respect to the Lord's return, *"For this they willingly are ignorant of…."* God was well aware of this condition in Jeremiah's day as well. *"Hear now this, O foolish people, and without understanding; which have eyes, and see not; which have ears, and hear not"* (Jeremiah 5:21).

Have you ever heard a parent say to his child, "Did you **hear** me?" The parent is not asking if the child physically heard what was said, but rather emphasizing whether or not the child was going to **obey** what was **heard**!

### B.  A Woeful Disaster

Disobedience never has a happy ending. Ask Adam, Cain, Achan, Samson, or Saul! Can you ever think of a time in your life when you disobeyed to your benefit? Someone has said, "It is a great deal easier to do that which God gives us to do, no matter how hard it is, than to face the responsibility of not doing it."

Samuel reminded King Saul of the disaster of disobedience in 1 Samuel 15:22–23, "…*Behold, to obey is better than sacrifice, and to hearken than the fat of rams. For rebellion is as the sin of witchcraft, and stubbornness is as iniquity and idolatry. Because thou hast rejected the word of the LORD, he hath also rejected thee from being king.*"

When I confronted him with his sin, a man once said to me, "Rule number one is that you always sin by yourself." His thought was, if you sin by yourself, no one will ever know. The truth is, however, that we never sin alone. Our sin affects not only us, but many others as well. Jonah's disobedience eventually brought about a storm that impacted many.

## III. Jonah's Nation

God has saved us and left us here on this earth for a reason.

"*Ye have not chosen me, but I have chosen you, and ordained you, that ye should go and bring forth fruit, and that your fruit should remain….*"—JOHN 15:16

*"For we are his workmanship, created in Christ Jesus unto good works, which God hath before ordained that we should walk in them."* —EPHESIANS 2:10

God didn't save you to sit, soak, and sour. He saved you to stand, strive, and serve!

### A. The Nemesis of Indifference

God reveals how repugnant apathy is when He scolds the church at Laodicea in Revelation 3:15–19: *"I know thy works, that thou art neither cold nor hot: I would thou wert cold or hot. So then because thou art lukewarm, and neither cold nor hot, I will spue thee out of my mouth. Because thou sayest, I am rich, and increased with goods, and have need of nothing; and knowest not that thou art wretched, and miserable, and poor, and blind, and naked: I counsel thee to buy of me gold tried in the fire, that thou mayest be rich; and white raiment, that thou mayest be clothed, and that the shame of thy nakedness do not appear; and anoint thine eyes with eyesalve, that thou mayest see. As many as I love, I rebuke and chasten: be zealous therefore, and repent."*

Archibald MacLeish said, "The crime against life, the worst of all crimes, is not to feel. And there was never, perhaps, a civilization in which that crime, the crime of torpor, of lethargy, of apathy, the snake-like sin of coldness-at-the-heart, was commoner than in our technical civilization."

Martin Niemoller stated, "In Germany they came first for the Communists, and I didn't speak up because I wasn't a Communist. Then they came for the Jews, and I didn't speak up because I wasn't a Jew. Then they came for the trade unionists, and I didn't speak up because I wasn't a trade unionist. Then they came for the Catholics, and I didn't speak up because I was a Protestant. Then they came for me, and by that time no one was left to speak up."

### B.  The Necessity of Involvement

In truth, we are our brothers' keepers! We are all missionaries, and every person we meet is a candidate for the Gospel.

*"When I say unto the wicked, O wicked man, thou shalt surely die; if thou dost not speak to warn the wicked from his way, that wicked man shall die in his iniquity; but his blood will I require at thine hand."*—EZEKIEL 33:8

The Great Commission is not a suggestion—it's a mandate! Like Jonah, we may not think that the world deserves the message, but we must remember that God loves the whole world! Every child of God is "an ambassador for Christ."

## IV. Jonah's Notoriety

Sadly, Jonah is remembered for his disobedience—not exactly what the average person wants on his resumé. If your life ended today, for what would you be remembered? Would there be people in Heaven because of you? Or, would there be people in Hell because of you?

### A.  A Legacy of Disobedience

People do not typically think of preaching or revival when they think of Jonah. In reality, however, perhaps the greatest revival in history took place under the preaching of Jonah as the entire city of Nineveh repented after one sermon! Still, we remember Jonah for his disobedience.

Obedience to God has long-range ramifications that are positive and productive, while disobedience leaves a tough stain that is rarely removed entirely. Isaiah 1:19–20 puts it well, *"If ye be willing and obedient, ye shall eat the good of the land: But if ye refuse and rebel, ye shall be devoured with the sword: for the mouth of the LORD hath spoken it."*

Before disobedience brings a legacy of disaster in our own lives, we would do well to heed the verse that precedes Isaiah's warning, *"Come now, and let us reason together, saith the LORD: though your sins be as scarlet, they shall be as white as snow; though they be red like crimson, they shall be as wool"* (Isaiah 1:18).

## B. A Lesson in Decisions

What can we learn from the life of Jonah? There is a law in life called "The Law of Cause and Effect." Nothing just happens. Every decision determines a direction, which leads to a destination. No one intends to end up in Hell. No one intends to ruin his life. No one accidentally ends up in Heaven or in the will of God.

You may not turn 180 degrees away from the will of God today, but making a decision that is just one degree away from complete obedience will cause you to miss God's best by miles in the end.

*"I call heaven and earth to record this day against you, that I have set before you life and death, blessing and cursing: therefore choose life, that both thou and thy seed may live: That thou mayest love the LORD thy God, and that thou mayest obey his voice, and that thou mayest*

*cleave unto him: for he is thy life, and the length of thy days: that thou mayest dwell in the land which the* LORD *sware unto thy fathers, to Abraham, to Isaac, and to Jacob, to give them."*—DEUTERONOMY 30:19–20

SECTION ONE

# A Sovereign Call

# A Call Revealed

## Key Verses

*"Now the word of the LORD came unto Jonah the son of Amittai, saying, Arise, go to Nineveh, that great city, and cry against it; for their wickedness is come up before me."*—JONAH 1:1–2

## Overview

It is not God's fault that sinners are lost and on their way to Hell. It is not God's fault that revival among God's people seems non-existent. God has called enough people to accomplish His work. The problem is not with the harvest— the problem is with the laborers! The problem is not with God's **voice**; the problem is with our **ears**!

## Lesson Theme

Two voices stand on the street corners of our lives: the voice of the world and the voice of wisdom. *"My son, if sinners entice thee, consent thou not…Wisdom crieth without; she uttereth her voice in the streets"* (Proverbs 1:10, 20). The end of Proverbs chapter one gives us the results of heeding these voices: *"For the turning away of the simple shall slay them, and the prosperity of fools shall destroy them. But whoso hearkeneth unto me shall dwell safely, and shall be quiet from fear of evil"* (Proverbs 1:32–33).

## Lesson Objectives

- To encourage the student to discern the voice of God and obey His voice.
- To help the student understand that as children of God, we do not have an option, but rather an obligation to serve the Lord.
- To create in the student a tenacity and boldness to speak God's message even when it is unpopular and may bring persecution.

## Teaching Outline

    I. A Commission of Authority
      A. God's Voice Discerned
      B. God's Vision Determined

   II. A Call for Action
      A. It's Time to Wake up
      B. It's Time to Walk
      C. It's Time to Warn

  III. A Communication of Agony
      A. An Elevated Position
      B. An Extreme Pollution
      C. An Expired Patience

# A Call Revealed

## Text

*"Now the word of the LORD came unto Jonah the son of Amittai, saying, Arise, go to Nineveh, that great city, and cry against it; for their wickedness is come up before me."*
—JONAH 1:1–2

In his book, *The Evangelist*, Dr. John R. Rice stated, "The trouble is not with the harvest but with the reapers. Men are lost but they can be saved. Hearts are hard but they can be broken with the Gospel. Sinners are blinded, sinners are enslaved by Satan, sinners are even dead in trespasses and sins, but Christ has opened blind eyes and released the captives and raised the dead before. Sinners are always lost, always hardened and blinded and enslaved. The basic facts about the power of the Gospel have never changed. Around the world, in all ages and all lands, the harvest has been white and the laborers few. The harvest is white today.... In any particular community there may be times of sowing and then times of reaping, an ebb and flow of opportunity. That has been true in all ages and it is not different today. But around the world it is continually the same: multitudes of people are ripe for the Gospel and could be won by Spirit-filled, impassioned and zealous soulwinners. The world is white to the harvest. It always has been and always will be as long as human hearts are what they are and sin is what it is and the Gospel is what it is. **There is not trouble with the harvest; the trouble is with the reapers**."

# I.   A Commission of Authority

Much of the problem today is that we do not allow God to be God in our lives. This is the problem stated in Romans 1:21, *"Because that, when they knew God, they glorified him not as God…."* We are like the people in 2 Kings 17:33 who *"feared the LORD, and served their own gods…."* Worse yet, we have made ourselves "gods" and like the people in the book of Judges, *"every man does that which was right in his own eyes"* (Judges 21:25).

## A.  God's Voice Discerned

Do you recognize God's voice? Can you pick it out in the midst of a world of voices shouting at you?

In Acts chapter nine, we find Saul of Tarsus on his way to Damascus to persecute any Christians he could find there. As he journeyed, *"he came near Damascus: and suddenly there shined round about him a light from heaven: And he fell to the earth, and heard a voice saying unto him, Saul, Saul, why persecutest thou me? And he said, Who art thou, **Lord**?"* He answered his own question!

You see, he had been hearing that voice for a long time. No doubt he heard it speaking to his heart at the stoning of Stephen in Acts chapter six.

A wise man or woman will have an ear that is attentive to God's voice and a heart that is eager to obey that voice. *"To day if ye will hear his voice, Harden not your heart…"* (Psalm 95:7–8).

## B. God's Vision Determined

Have you ever met someone who talks because he is nervous or because he is uneasy with silence? He doesn't have much to say, other than a lot of "idle" chatter! This is never the case with God. When God speaks, He does so with a purpose. He has carefully crafted His message, and every word is essential!

Verse one of Jonah tells us that *"the word of the Lord came unto Jonah."* This was God's message to His child. It was not to be ignored.

There is nothing more frustrating than being in the middle of an important conversation with someone on the phone when suddenly the call is "dropped."

Make sure your spiritual battery is always charged. Be sure to stay "close" to God—that is, in "range"—so that His call in your life is not "dropped."

*"How do ye say, We are wise, and the law of the Lord is with us? Lo, certainly in vain made he it; the pen of the scribes is in vain. The wise men are ashamed, they are dismayed and taken: lo, they have rejected the word of the Lord; and what wisdom is in them?"*—JEREMIAH 8:8–9

## II. A Call for Action

Three "action" words are found in verse two: arise, go, and cry. Theory never gets the job done. First John 3:18 states, *"My little children, let us not love in word, neither in tongue; but in deed and in truth."* In John 13:17, Jesus reminds us, *"If ye **know** these things, happy are ye if ye **do** them."*

### A. *It's Time to Wake Up*

Someone has wisely stated, "The church is a sleeping giant." We have all of the power of the universe on our side, but we have fallen asleep. *"His watchmen are blind: they are all ignorant, they are all dumb dogs, they cannot bark; sleeping, lying down, loving to slumber"* (Isaiah 56:10).

The Apostle Paul set the alarm clock in Romans 13:11–12: *"And that, knowing the time, that now it is high time to awake out of sleep: for now is our salvation nearer than when we believed. The night is far spent, the day is at hand: let us therefore cast off the works of darkness, and let us put on the armour of light."*

### B. *It's Time to Walk*

Interestingly, in Romans 13:13–14, Paul adds this challenge to his call to awaken: *"Let us walk honestly, as in the day; not in rioting and drunkenness, not in chambering and wantonness, not in strife and envying. But put ye on the Lord Jesus Christ, and make not provision for the flesh, to fulfil the lusts thereof."*

We must awaken to God's message of truth, but we must also practice that truth.

No one will listen to us if we do not live what we preach. In Ephesians 4:1, we are told, *"I therefore, the prisoner of the Lord, beseech you that ye walk worthy of the vocation wherewith ye are called."*

Before we **warn** others of the error of the old sinful life, we must **walk** "in newness of life."

### C. It's Time to Warn

A doctor who never speaks to his patients about their eating habits or lack of exercise is not concerned about cancer or heart disease. Even so, we must warn others about their sin if we are truly concerned about their souls. Isaiah 58:1 says, *"Cry aloud, spare not, lift up thy voice like a trumpet, and shew my people their transgression, and the house of Jacob their sins."*

It may not be your personality to be negative or to warn people about their sin.

It may take you out of your comfort zone. Your motive however, should be a love for God and people. Remember what Christ said to the church at Laodicea? *"As many as I love, I rebuke and chasten: be zealous therefore, and repent"* (Revelation 3:19).

Someone once said, "It is better to build a fence at the top of a cliff than to park an ambulance below!"

# III. A Communication of Agony

Verse two of Jonah states that the wickedness of Nineveh had come up before the Lord. Their sin affected God and somebody needed to tell them. God's declaration was not a positive message that needed to be delivered. God's message is often spoken through the tears of a broken heart.

*"Oh that my head were waters, and mine eyes a fountain of tears, that I might weep day and night for the slain of the daughter of my people!"*—JEREMIAH 9:1

*"O Jerusalem, Jerusalem, thou that killest the prophets, and stonest them which are sent unto thee, how often would I have gathered thy children together, even as a hen gathereth her chickens under her wings, and ye would not."*—MATTHEW 23:37

## A. An Elevated Position

The Bible speaks of Nineveh as a "great" city in Jonah 1:2. This was certainly a reference to her size, but also to her influence. Often, God's blessings are taken for granted. When things are going well, we think that we don't need God. But Paul reminds us in 1 Corinthians 4:7, *"For who maketh thee to differ from another? and what hast thou that thou didst not receive? now if thou didst receive it, why dost thou glory, as if thou hadst not received it?"*

Moses feared amnesia among the people of Israel. He did not want them to forget the Lord in times of abundant blessing. We see this clearly stated in Deuteronomy 8:11–14, *"Beware that thou forget not the LORD thy God, in not keeping his commandments, and his judgments, and his statutes, which I command thee this day: Lest when thou hast eaten and art full, and hast built goodly houses, and dwelt therein; And when thy herds and thy flocks multiply, and thy silver and thy gold is multiplied, and all that thou hast is multiplied; Then thine heart be lifted up, and thou forget the LORD thy God, which brought thee forth out of the land of Egypt, from the house of bondage."*

Everything we possess is a gift from God and is never to be taken lightly. Sometimes, the more God blesses—the greater target of Satan we become. Therefore, it behooves us *"to do justly, and to love mercy, and to walk humbly with thy God"* (Micah 6:8).

## B. An Extreme Pollution

Man's wickedness had come up to the presence of God. Sin is present in every society, but there are times when the stench of that sin reaches the nostrils of God in an unusually nauseating way. In Amos 5:12, God says, *"For I know your manifold transgressions and your mighty sins…."*

Now, be careful! It is easy to excuse ourselves here as not being as bad as the people of Nineveh. But keep in mind *"that a little leaven leaveneth the whole lump."* God is absolutely pure. Just a "little" sin in our lives will pollute His presence.

## C. An Expired Patience

God is a patient, merciful, and long-suffering God. Psalm 103:8 says, *"The LORD is merciful and gracious, slow to anger, and plenteous in mercy."* However, the very next verse states, *"He will not always chide: neither will he keep his anger for ever."* Is God convicting you of some sin today? Don't try His patience.

Proverbs 28:13 says, *"He that covereth his sins shall not prosper: but whoso confesseth and forsaketh them shall have mercy."* Sin has a medium of exchange that trades in sorrow, disillusionment, and death. Christ can forgive any trespass—He can overlook none. Forgiveness is man's deepest need and highest achievement. Reamer

Loomis said, "The wages of sin is death—thank God I quit before payday!"

# A Common Rebellion

## Key Verse

*"But Jonah rose up to flee unto Tarshish from the presence of the LORD, and went down to Joppa; and he found a ship going to Tarshish: so he paid the fare thereof, and went down into it, to go with them unto Tarshish from the presence of the LORD."*
—JONAH 1:3

## Overview

It seems to be part of our human nature to "ignore the sermon and wait for the siren." Man somehow thinks that he will be the exception to the rule, or that God isn't really serious about His commands. Sometimes, God will let us go our way in order to teach us a lesson the hard way. Experience is not the best teacher, (the Holy Spirit is) but experience is a very **effective** teacher!

## Lesson Theme

God has created us with the ability to choose. While the choice is ours, the consequence of that choice is not. Lessons are often learned in the "school of hard knocks" but there is often a steep price that becomes part of our "permanent records."

# Lesson Objectives

- To help the student understand rebellion as a part of his old sinful natures.
- To cause the student to evaluate carefully every choice that is set before him.
- To enable the student to realize that any choice made against God's plan will always lead to ruin.
- To challenge the student to make wise choices in life that will lead to God's blessing and his benefit.

# Teaching Outline

I. An Attempt to Flee
   A. A Human Inclination
   B. A Hopeless Impossibility

II. An Alternative Is Found
   A. An Obstinate Decision
   B. An Opposite Direction

III. An Agreement on the Fare
   A. Every Decision Has a Price
   B. Every Decision Has a Purchase Order

# A Common Rebellion

## Text

*"But Jonah rose up to flee unto Tarshish from the presence of the LORD, and went down to Joppa; and he found a ship going to Tarshish: so he paid the fare thereof, and went down into it, to go with them unto Tarshish from the presence of the LORD."*
—JONAH 1:3

Perhaps you have heard the expression, "We are all different." While it is true that every one of us is unique (which is probably a good thing), we are very similar in our human makeup. We are *all* made in God's image, but at the same time, we have *all* sinned and come short of the glory of God. All of us have a weakened and sinful flesh, but we also can yield our lives to the Holy Spirit and have God's power working in and through us as a result.

One of the reasons Jonah is such a popular character in the Bible is that while we hate to admit it, we see ourselves in his life. While rebellion may be a common human characteristic, the result of that rebellion is also going to be the same. Therefore, we need to learn from Jonah's mistakes and take a different course of action.

# I.   An Attempt to Flee

Verse three states that, *"Jonah rose up to flee unto Tarshish from the presence of the LORD."* Honest confession is not our first thought when we sin. Our flesh wants to find an excuse or an escape. We hope there will be no ramification to our disobedience, but such is never the case. Someone has said, "Sin is the world's best detective—it always finds you out!"

## A.  A Human Inclination

No doubt we are all familiar with Adam and Eve's sin in the garden of Eden. Notice what happened right after they sinned in Genesis 3:7–8: *"And the eyes of them both were opened, and they knew that they were naked; and they sewed fig leaves together, and made themselves aprons. And they heard the voice of the LORD God walking in the garden in the cool of the day: and Adam and his wife hid themselves from the presence of the LORD God amongst the trees of the garden."*

The first reaction of Adam and Eve was to run from the presence of God. Man has been running from his sin ever since.

## B.  A Hopeless Impossibility

Jeremiah 23:24 asks, *"Can any hide himself in secret places that I shall not see him? saith the LORD. Do not I fill heaven and earth? saith the LORD."* The Psalmist asks a similar question and finds the same answer in Psalm 139:7–12: *"Whither shall I go from thy spirit? or whither shall I flee from thy presence? If I ascend up into heaven, thou art there: if I make my bed in hell, behold, thou art there. If I take the wings of the morning, and dwell in the uttermost parts of the sea; Even there shall thy hand lead me, and thy right hand shall hold me. If I say, Surely the darkness shall cover me; even the night shall be light about me. Yea, the darkness hideth not from thee; but the night shineth as the day: the darkness and the light are both alike to thee."*

Sometimes teenagers say, "When I'm eighteen, I'm out of here!" While you may be legally on your own when you turn a certain age, where can you go where God isn't already there? In which city, or state, or on which planet will you live where God does not exist? The prodigal son left home, but God never left him alone. God was just as much alive and well under the bright lights of sin in the far country as He had ever been under the rules and regulations of his father's house.

## II. An Alternative Is Found

In the middle of verse three we read these words, *"…and he found a ship going to Tarshish…."* Satan will make sure that there is always a ship going the opposite direction of God's will in your life. He makes sure there are lots of choices besides that of obedience. And amazingly, we often find it so "coincidental" that there is an alternative to doing right. We can even "spiritualize" the seemingly "open door" that lies before us.

Eve reasoned that this forbidden tree *"was good for food, and that it was pleasant to the eyes, and a tree to be desired to make one wise…"* (Genesis 3:6). Lot lifted up his eyes, *"and beheld all the plain of Jordan, that it was well watered every where, before the LORD destroyed Sodom and Gomorrah, even as the garden of the LORD, like the land of Egypt, as thou comest unto Zoar"* (Genesis 13:10). Achan confessed in Joshua 7:21, *"When I saw among the spoils a goodly Babylonish garment, and two hundred shekels of silver, and a wedge of gold of fifty shekels weight, then I coveted them, and took them…."*

Satan's alternatives are always attractive, for it is his goal to be the perfect counterfeit of Christ. Paul warns us about Satan's tactics in 2 Corinthians 11:13–15, *"For such are false apostles, deceitful workers, transforming themselves into the apostles of Christ. And no marvel; for Satan himself is transformed into an angel of light. Therefore it is no great thing if his ministers also be transformed as the ministers of righteousness; whose end shall be according to their works."*

## A. An Obstinate Decision

When we make a decision that is in violation to God's will for our lives, we are saying to God that we as the creatures are smarter than the Creator. In Romans 9:20, Paul asks, *"Nay but, O man, who art thou that repliest against God? Shall the thing formed say to him that formed it, Why hast thou made me thus?"*

Job of old offers some wise counsel in Job 9:2–4, *"I know it is so of a truth: but how should man be just with God? If he will contend with him, he cannot answer him one of a thousand. He is wise in heart, and mighty in strength: who hath hardened himself against him, and hath prospered?"*

### B. An Opposite Direction

In verse three, the Bible says that Jonah fled from the presence of the Lord, and *"went **down** to Joppa."* Any direction away from God's will is always *down*! By the way, once you head down, the trip up is a lot more difficult. Later in verse three it says that he *"went **down** into it"* (the ship). By the time we see him in verse five, he has *"gone **down** into the sides of the ship."* Once you start going down there is a momentum that is difficult to reverse. It took a very sick fish for Jonah to start heading back *up*!

# III. An Agreement on the Fare

Once Jonah found an alternative (the devil always makes sure there is a ship in port that is headed the opposite direction of God's will for your life), it says in verse three, *"… so he paid the fare thereof."*

Amazingly, none of us want to pay the wages *of* sin, but we are willing to pay the wages *to* sin! We don't like it when the preacher tells us that there is a "cost" to serving God with our lives, but we are willing to pay the "cost" to run from that service!

### A. Every Decision Has a Price

By the time we get to 2 Samuel 24, David has paid a great price for his sin. Every time he had disobeyed God, it had cost him dearly. A little seven-day-old baby had died; Uriah had died; David's sons had died; and now, because he had numbered the people, 70,000 of his men had died (2 Samuel 24:15). That's a pretty hefty "fare" for sin, wouldn't you say?

God instructs David through Gad to build an altar and offer a sacrifice to the Lord at the threshing floor of Araunah, the Jebusite. Araunah is willing to give David the threshing floor along with the oxen and the threshing instruments. But by this time, David has learned that every decision, both good and bad, has a price. In verse twenty-four of 2 Samuel 24, David responds to Araunah's offer as follows: *"And the king said unto Araunah, Nay; but I will surely buy it of thee at a price: neither will I offer burnt offerings unto the LORD my God of that which doth cost me nothing. So David bought the threshingfloor and the oxen for fifty shekels of silver."*

We all know that there is a price to be paid for sin. That price often looks like a good deal—but the product we receive is death! *"For the wages of sin is death…"* (Romans 6:23). Jesus spoke of the price of service in Matthew 10:38, *"And he that taketh not his cross, and followeth after me, is not worthy of me."* Often, that price of service doesn't look attractive to us, but verses thirty-nine and following speak of the "product" of that price, *"He that findeth his life shall lose it: and he that loseth his life for my sake shall find it."* In Mark 10:29–30, He reiterates this message, *"Verily I say unto you, There is no man that hath left house, or brethren, or sisters, or father, or mother, or wife, or children, or lands, for my sake, and the gospel's, But he shall receive an hundredfold now in this time, houses, and brethren, and sisters, and mothers, and children, and lands, with persecutions; and in the world to come eternal life."*

### B. Every Decision Has a Purchase Order

Purchase orders are essential if an organization is to stay within budgetary restrictions. They enable us to make wise decisions with respect to the money we have or don't have.

It is interesting that God has made human beings with an ability to delay a decision. Animals do not have this same capability—they simply react to a stimulus. That is why a dog may even bite his owner, because he does not possess this ability to "think" through a decision before it is made.

Temptation is a part of every person's life. Jesus was tempted in all points as we are, according to Hebrews 4:15, and yet without sin. By His grace and enabling, He gives us that same potential: *"There hath no temptation taken you but such as is common to man: but God is faithful, who will not suffer you to be tempted above that ye are able; but will with the temptation also make a way to escape, that ye may be able to bear it"* (1 Corinthians 10:13).

The next time you are tempted to live contrary to God's direction—before you pay the "fare," stop and think for a minute. You are about to sign a purchase order for a product. What kind of product do you want? *"The Lord knoweth how to deliver the godly out of temptations, and to reserve the unjust unto the day of judgment to be punished"* (2 Peter 2:9). Either way, you will pay—make sure your decision is worth the price!

# A Countering Rebuke

## Key Verses

*"But the LORD sent out a great wind into the sea, and there was a mighty tempest in the sea, so that the ship was like to be broken. Then the mariners were afraid, and cried every man unto his god, and cast forth the wares that were in the ship into the sea, to lighten it of them. But Jonah was gone down into the sides of the ship; and he lay, and was fast asleep. So the shipmaster came to him, and said unto him, What meanest thou, O sleeper? arise, call upon thy God, if so be that God will think upon us, that we perish not. And they said every one to his fellow, Come, and let us cast lots, that we may know for whose cause this evil is upon us. So they cast lots, and the lot fell upon Jonah. Then said they unto him, Tell us, we pray thee, for whose cause this evil is upon us; What is thine occupation? and whence comest thou? what is thy country? and of what people are thou? And he said unto them, I am an Hebrew; and I fear the LORD, the God of heaven, which hath made the sea and the dry land. Then were the men exceedingly afraid, and said unto him, Why hast thou done this? For the men knew that he fled from the presence of the LORD, because he had told them."—*JONAH 1:4–10

## Overview

God never sits idly by as we make wrong decisions. He is a loving Father who cares greatly for us and doesn't want us to get hurt by our sin. The wise person will make a U-turn at the first warning sign He gives. *"A fool despiseth his father's instruction: but he that regardeth reproof is prudent"* (Proverbs 15:5).

## Lesson Theme

Rebellion and stubbornness are wicked sins (see 1 Samuel 15:23). We will all make bad decisions along the way in life, but how we respond to those bad decisions is important. When God speaks to us after the decision is made, do we "dig in" our heels to prove that we can win without God, or are we attentive to God's correction? *"For whom the Lord loveth he chasteneth, and scourgeth every son whom he receiveth"* (Hebrews 12:6).

## Lesson Objectives

- To help the student realize that God loves us even when we make bad choices and will intersect our path in order to correct us.
- To encourage the student to respond to God's first correction, lest that chastening become more severe.
- To show the student that there is a price to be paid for every step taken down the wrong path. We may eventually turn around and get right—but at what cost?
- To enable the student to see that in the course of disobedience we do great damage to the testimony of Christ.

## Teaching Outline

I.  The Blasting of the Storm
    A.  An Omnipotent Creator
    B.  An Over-powering Circumstance

II. The Breaking of the Ship
    A. Man's Refuge Is Vulnerable
    B. Man's Resolve Is Vain

III. The Burden of Sin
    A. A Careless Indifference
    B. A Costly Iniquity

IV. The Belittling of the Sacred
    A. An Honest Confession
    B. A Horrible Confusion

# A Countering Rebuke

## Text

*"But the LORD sent out a great wind into the sea, and there was a mighty tempest in the sea, so that the ship was like to be broken. Then the mariners were afraid, and cried every man unto his god, and cast forth the wares that were in the ship into the sea, to lighten it of them. But Jonah was gone down into the sides of the ship; and he lay, and was fast asleep. So the shipmaster came to him, and said unto him, What meanest thou, O sleeper? arise, call upon thy God, if so be that God will think upon us, that we perish not. And they said every one to his fellow, Come, and let us cast lots, that we may know for whose cause this evil is upon us. So they cast lots, and the lot fell upon Jonah. Then said they unto him, Tell us, we pray thee, for whose cause this evil is upon us; What is thine occupation? and whence comest thou? what is thy country? and of what people are thou? And he said unto them, I am an Hebrew; and I fear the LORD, the God of heaven, which hath made the sea*

*and the dry land. Then were the men exceedingly afraid, and said unto him, Why hast thou done this? For the men knew that he fled from the presence of the LORD, because he had told them."*—JONAH 1:4–10

God will not let you go "down" without a fight! His intense love for you will go the extra mile to keep you from ruining your life, as well as the lives of others. Hebrews 12:6 reminds us, *"For whom the Lord loveth he chasteneth, and scourgeth every son whom he receiveth."* No one likes to be told that they are wrong, or worse yet, be chastened in the process, but verse eleven of the same chapter goes on to say, *"Now no chastening for the present seemeth to be joyous, but grievous: nevertheless afterward it yieldeth the peaceable fruit of righteousness unto them which are exercised thereby."*

In David's case, he stated in Psalm 51, *"my sin is ever before me"* (verse 3). God has a way of reminding us that we are going a wrong direction. It is the Holy Spirit's "job" to "reprove the world of sin" and He is certainly capable of reproving us as well.

At this point, Jonah is not very sensitive to the reproof of God. Because he has been saying "no" to God for quite some time, his conscience has become dulled and his sensitivity to the still small voice of God has been lost. Thus, God has to get out the "big lumber" so to speak. Deliberate disobedience calls for drastic discipline!

## I.   The Blasting of the Storm

Jonah 1:4 states, *"But the LORD sent out a great wind into the sea, and there was a mighty tempest in the sea."*

Not every storm or trial in our lives is a result of sin. Jesus suffered as no human being ever has—not because He was wrong, but because He was right! There are numerous examples in Scripture of men who endured great trials (Job, Daniel, Joseph, Paul), but there is no evidence that these storms were a result of sin in their lives. Storms often make God's children stronger or simply provide opportunities to glorify God.

However, there is nothing that gets our attention any quicker than a trial. It is often in these great crises that our only hope is to turn back to God. Because God created us for His pleasure and fellowship, He is willing in His love for us to use a storm to bring us back home to His will.

### A. An Omnipotent Creator

Notice the phrase *"But the LORD"* (Jonah 1:4). Aren't you glad that God still loves us even when we go astray? Revelation 4:11 states, *"…for thou hast created all things, and for thy pleasure they are and were created."* When our lives no longer bring pleasure to God, He is willing to do whatever is necessary to bring us back to a place where we can be pleasing to Him.

To do that, God has all of creation at His disposal! Psalm 119:90–91 states, *"Thy faithfulness is unto all generations: thou hast established the earth, and it abideth. They continue this day according to thine ordinances: for all are thy servants."* Everything that God made is His servant. Yes, He can make a rooster crow at the right time to convict a Peter, or a donkey balk to convict a Balaam, or a whale to swallow a Jonah. (More on that later!)

They said of Jesus, *"What manner of man is this, that even the winds and the sea obey him!"* (Matthew 8:27). As the old song says, "He's got the whole world in His hands!"

## B. An Over-powering Circumstance

When we fight against God—we will always lose! Fighting God is like trying to win a war against laser guided missiles with laser tag guns. Hannah's prayer in 1 Samuel 2:2–9 reminds us of God's power over creation circumstances: *"There is none holy as the LORD: for there is none beside thee: neither is there any rock like our God. Talk no more so exceeding proudly; let not arrogancy come out of your mouth: for the LORD is a God of knowledge, and by him actions are weighed. The bows of the mighty men are broken, and they that stumbled are girded with strength. They that were full have hired out themselves for bread; and they that were hungry ceased: so that the barren hath born seven; and she that hath many children is waxed feeble. The LORD killeth, and maketh alive: he bringeth down to the grave, and bringeth up. The LORD maketh poor, and maketh rich: he bringeth low, and lifteth up. He raiseth up the poor out of the dust, and lifteth up the beggar from the dunghill, to set them among princes, and to make them inherit the throne of glory: for the pillars of the earth are the LORD's, and he hath set the world upon them. He will keep the feet of his saints, and the wicked shall be silent in darkness; for by strength shall no man prevail."*

Job asked, *"…Who hath hardened himself against him, and hath prospered?"* (Job 9:4). The warning of Isaiah is sufficient here, *"Woe unto him that striveth with his Maker!"* (Isaiah 45:9).

# II.  The Breaking of the Ship

When Jonah heard the wind howling and felt the rain falling, he should have retreated. Unfortunately, he wasn't on the deck of the ship to see any lightening bolts.

Jonah was set on his disobedience, so it took more than the storm to get his attention. Had the storm gotten his attention—all that would have been broken was his will, but now the damage was more severe. Verse four ends with this phrase, "…*the ship was like to be broken.*"

### A. Man's Refuge Is Vulnerable

Where was Jonah during the storm? Was he huddled with the other mariners watching the skies for a break in the weather? Was he seeking advice from the captain of the ship? No. Verse five says, "*But Jonah was gone down into the sides of the ship…and was fast asleep.*"

It seems he was oblivious to what was taking place and simply didn't care. He found refuge in his disobedience and was resolved to ride out the consequences. Sin's refuge is a lousy counterfeit to the Saviour's redemption. Man thinks he is happy without God, but the psalmist wisely advises us to, "*…taste and see that the LORD is good: blessed is the man that trusteth in him*" (Psalm 34:8).

The lost sinner finds refuge in his religion and good works—but he is vulnerable. It is "*Not by works of righteousness which we have done, but according to his mercy he saved us, by the washing of regeneration, and renewing of the Holy Ghost; Which he shed on us abundantly through Jesus Christ our Saviour*" (Titus 3:5–6).

As Christians, we may find refuge in our way, but God declares, "*My thoughts are not your thoughts, neither are your ways my ways, saith the LORD. For as the heavens are higher than the earth, so are my ways higher than your ways, and my thoughts than your thoughts*" (Isaiah 55:8–9). Yes, "*there is a way which seemeth right unto a man, but the end thereof are the ways of death*" (Proverbs 14:12).

### B. *Man's Resolve Is Vain*

In verse five, the mariners on board this ship realized they were in trouble. They tried everything to alleviate this problem. *"Then the mariners were afraid, and cried every man unto his god, and cast forth the wares that were in the ship into the sea, to lighten it of them…."*

Amazingly, man tries to solve his problems without God. Paul poured out his heart to God concerning His people in Romans 10:1–3: *"Brethren, my heart's desire and prayer to God for Israel is, that they might be saved. For I bear them record that they have a zeal of God, but not according to knowledge. For they being ignorant of God's righteousness, and going about to establish their own righteousness, have not submitted themselves unto the righteousness of God."* The children of Israel were trying to solve their own problems.

"Submitted" is the operative word in that passage of Romans. That's all it takes to get saved! Submit to what God has already done for you! That's all it takes to be obedient! *"Trust in the Lord with all thine heart; and lean not unto thine own understanding. In all thy ways acknowledge him, and he shall direct thy paths"* (Proverbs 3:5–6).

It's not rocket science, as they say. It's pretty simple, but it seems to be human nature to wait for a few boards to come off the ship before we wake up!

## III. The Burden of Sin

Sin has a lot of heavy baggage! I suppose the world might say that it is hard to live the Christian life. While there are times when it may not be easy, what does the Bible say? *"Come unto me, all ye that labour and are heavy laden, and*

*I will give you rest. Take my yoke upon you, and learn of me; for I am meek and lowly in heart: and ye shall find rest unto your souls. For my yoke is easy, and my burden is light"* (Matthew 11:28–30). On the other side of that coin, God declares that the *"way of transgressors is hard"* (Proverbs 13:15). *"But the wicked are like the troubled sea, when it cannot rest, whose waters cast up mire and dirt. There is no peace, saith my God, to the wicked"* (Isaiah 57:20–21).

## A.  A Careless Indifference

As we saw earlier, Jonah is fast asleep in the sides of the ship (verse 5). I have watched people in hospital waiting rooms and funeral parlors who still don't get it! Their sin has caused heartache, sorrow, sickness, and even death, but they still don't care.

Sin has a way of blinding us to the truth. *"We grope for the wall like the blind, and we grope as if we had no eyes: we stumble at noon day as in the night; we are in desolate places as dead men"* (Isaiah 59:10). Paul reminds us that our understanding of spiritual things can be diminished by sin: *"Having the understanding darkened, being alienated from the life of God through the ignorance that is in them, because of the blindness of their heart"* (Ephesians 4:18).

Like those in Laodicea, we can assume that we are *"rich, and increased with goods, and have need of nothing; and knowest not that thou art wretched, and miserable, and poor, and blind and naked"* (Revelation 3:17).

## B.  A Costly Iniquity

Carelessness never eliminates cost! We can stick our heads in the sand and hope God goes away, but a holy

God cannot tolerate unholiness in His people. Sadly, our sin affects others. (David's baby died, his sons died, Uriah died, and many of his men died.) In verse six of Jonah chapter one we read, *"So the shipmaster came to him, and said unto him, What meanest thou, O sleeper? arise, call upon thy God, if so be that God will think upon us, that we perish not."* Jonah's careless indifference affected the others on the ship.

The damage from an earthquake is not limited to the epicenter. Years ago, a pastor friend of mine and I went to a bar late at night on Long Island, New York to find the husband of a Christian lady. At about one in the morning we located him and got him to step outside. We pleaded with him to come home to his family but to no avail. Finally, he stepped out into the street and stood in the midst of on-rushing cars, looked up into the rain falling from the sky and said, "Go ahead and kill me God!" After not dying in the next five seconds, he came over and said to me, "See, there ain't no God!" I looked him in the eyes and said, "God's not going to kill you— you aren't worth killing! But He might just kill your little two-year-old daughter if you don't straighten up." That man sobered up instantly, came home with us, and was in church the next night! The realization of the cost of his iniquity caused him to cease from indifference!

Jonah's disobedience could have cost some men their lives, some wives their husbands, and some little children back home in Joppa their daddies. Be sure that your sin isn't costing you eternity, or your family, or your ministry. That's way too steep a price to pay for a boat ride from Joppa to Tarshish!

# IV. The Belittling of the Sacred

Because we are selfish by nature, we only think of the personal ramifications to our sin. What often escapes our responsibility is the effect that our sin has on God! Peter reminds us, *"But ye are a chosen generation, a royal priesthood, an holy nation, a peculiar people; that ye should shew forth the praises of him who hath called you out of darkness into his marvellous light: Which in time past were not a people, but are now the people of God: which had not obtained mercy, but now have obtained mercy. Dearly beloved, I beseech you as strangers and pilgrims, abstain from fleshly lusts, which war against the soul; Having your conversation honest among the Gentiles: that, whereas they speak against you as evildoers, they may by your good works, which they shall behold, glorify God in the day of visitation"* (1 Peter 2:9–12).

Most people never read a Bible—but they read our lives every day! *"Ye are our epistle written in our hearts, known and read of all men. Forasmuch as ye are manifestly declared to be the epistle of Christ ministered by us, written not with ink, but with the Spirit of the living God; not in tables of stone, but in fleshy tables of the heart"* (2 Corinthians 3:2–3). Paul warns us, *"Giving no offence in any thing, that the ministry be not blamed"* (2 Corinthians 6:3).

## A. An Honest Confession

Finally, in verse nine, Jonah gets honest: *"…I am an Hebrew; and I fear the LORD, the God of heaven, which hath made the sea and the dry land."*

Every "U-Turn" made in the direction of God starts with honesty. Proverbs 16:6 says, *"By mercy and truth iniquity is purged…."* And we might as well be honest since God knows the truth anyway. *"Neither is there any creature that is not manifest in his sight: but all things are naked and opened unto the eyes of him with whom we have to do"* (Hebrews 4:13).

Honesty is a wise policy all of the time. *"Providing for honest things, not only in the sight of the Lord, but also in the sight of men"* (2 Corinthians 8:21). Paul asks in Hebrews 13:18, *"Pray for us: for we trust we have a good conscience, in all things willing to live honestly."*

### B.  A Horrible Confusion

When Jonah reveals to these men who he is, they have a hard time understanding his disobedience. *"Then were the men exceedingly afraid, and said unto him, Why hast thou done this? For the men knew that he fled from the presence of the LORD, because he had told them"* (Jonah 1:10).

Years ago, Dr. Bill Rice was preaching a revival meeting in a small town. He and his family were staying near the church and, one night after preaching, his wife informed him that they needed a couple of items from the store. He grabbed his wallet and the list and headed to a corner market just a couple of blocks down the street. He entered the store and grabbed a loaf of bread and a gallon of milk and placed them on the check-out counter. The lady at the register reached down under the counter and pulled out a Playboy magazine and placed it on the counter in front of the evangelist. She said, "Would you like anything else, sir?" Dr. Rice, seeing the magazine and realizing what it was, quickly fixed his eyes on the lady and said, "No ma'am." She pushed the magazine a little closer to him and said, "Are you sure?" Without changing his gaze, he emphatically said, "Yes, I'm sure. How much is the bread and the milk, please?" The lady placed the magazine back under the counter, added the price of the two items and gave him the total. He paid her the money, received his change, grabbed the bag of groceries and headed for the door. As he reached for the door, the lady said, "Have a good evening, Evangelist Rice!" She had been in the service that night, had heard him preach, and decided to put him to the test. Thank God—he passed! But I wonder how many times we have failed a test like that, and no one has ever told us our grade? They just "chalked it up" as another Christian hypocrite.

David is reminded by Nathan that his sin had *"given great occasion to the enemies of the LORD to blaspheme..."* (2 Samuel 12:14). Let's not be guilty of Paul's warning in Romans 2:24, *"For the name of God is blasphemed among the Gentiles through you...."* The world has enough excuses for not trusting in Christ. Let's not let our lives add to their lists!

# A Chastisement Revival

## Key Verses

*"Then said they unto him, What shall we do unto thee, that the sea may be calm unto us? for the sea wrought, and was tempestuous. And he said unto them, Take me up, and cast me forth into the sea; so shall the sea be calm unto you: for I know that for my sake this great tempest is upon you. Nevertheless the men rowed hard to bring it to the land; but they could not: for the sea wrought, and was tempestuous against them. Wherefore they cried unto the LORD, and said, We beseech thee, O LORD, we beseech thee, let us not perish for this man's life, and lay not upon us innocent blood: for thou, O LORD, hast done as it pleased thee. So they took up Jonah, and cast him forth into the sea: and the sea ceased from her raging. Then the men feared the LORD exceedingly, and offered a sacrifice unto the LORD, and made vows."—JONAH 1:11–16*

## Overview

When you trace the history of revivals, you will find that they often started as a result of a crisis. The death of a prominent person, a financial crash, or natural disaster have often caused people to turn back to God. Human nature is what it is and often while we may sleep through the sermon, we are awakened by the siren.

# Lesson Theme

Chastisement is never pleasant, but it can bring about God's desired results in our lives. Second Corinthians 7:9–10 says, *"Now I rejoice, not that ye were made sorry, but that ye sorrowed to repentance: for ye were made sorry after a godly manner... For godly sorrow worketh repentance to salvation not to be repented of...."*

# Lesson Objectives

- To show the student that sometimes it is chastisement that God uses to get our attention.
- To help the student understand that God's goal in chastisement is always restoration rather than simply punishment.
- To challenge the student to make serious life-long vows that, when carried out, will bring God's blessing and power.

# Teaching Outline

I. A Sobered Reverence
   A. A Fearful Conversation
   B. A Fatal Conclusion

II. A Sacrificial Reconciliation
   A. The Effort of Man
   B. The Elusiveness of Mercy

III. A Surrendered Resolve
   A. A Serious Moment
   B. A Supernatural Miracle

# A Chastisement Revival

## Text

*"Then said they unto him, What shall we do unto thee, that the sea may be calm unto us? for the sea wrought, and was tempestuous. And he said unto them, Take me up, and cast me forth into the sea; so shall the sea be calm unto you: for I know that for my sake this great tempest is upon you. Nevertheless the men rowed hard to bring it to the land; but they could not: for the sea wrought, and was tempestuous against them. Wherefore they cried unto the LORD, and said, We beseech thee, O LORD, we beseech thee, let us not perish for this man's life, and lay not upon us innocent blood: for thou, O LORD, hast done as it pleased thee. So they took up Jonah, and cast him forth into the sea: and the sea ceased from her raging. Then the men feared the LORD exceedingly, and offered a sacrifice unto the LORD, and made vows."*—JONAH 1:11–16

When you read the account in Jonah 1:11–16, you get the impression that these mariners had been going to church all of their lives. Such was not the case, I believe. The power of God, however, was seen clearly perhaps for the first time in their lives and they knew that they were in a serious condition.

Revival often starts as a result of a trial. Jonathan Edwards pointed to the death of a prominent woman as the beginning of God's mighty work during the first Great Awakening. The famous "Prayer Meeting Revival" of the middle 1800s was spurred in part by the financial crisis of the hour. The great missionary endeavor of William Carey gained support following a fire that destroyed the printing press and much of Carey's early translation work.

The truth is, people get saved at funerals, in hospital waiting rooms, and in foxholes on war-torn battlefields. We all pray longer and harder when we are down to our last dollar or when our children are sick.

# I. A Sobered Reverence

By the time we reach verse sixteen, the demeanor of those on board this boat has drastically changed. *"Then the men feared the LORD exceedingly…."* What brought about this humility and hunger for God? Looking back through the story, we can come to some conclusions about their sudden interest in spiritual things.

## A. A Fearful Conversation

Verses nine through eleven record an interesting conversation between Jonah and these mariners, *"And he said unto them, I am an Hebrew; and I fear the LORD, the*

*God of heaven, which hath made the sea and the dry land. Then were the men exceedingly afraid, and said unto him, Why hast thou done this? For the men knew that he fled from the presence of the LORD, because he had told them. Then said they unto him, What shall we do unto thee, that the sea may be calm unto us? for the sea wrought, and was tempestuous."*

This is no ordinary storm. They are now fully aware that they are in the middle of God's judgment in a flimsy boat! The truth is, we're not safe in a submarine when God is at the throttle of the storm! The thief on the cross recognized the trouble he was in when he said to his partner in crime, *"...Dost not thou fear God, seeing thou art in the same condemnation? And we indeed justly; for we receive the due reward of our deeds..."* (Luke 23:40–41).

Often when we sin, we fear getting caught or perhaps paying the consequences of our sin. Matthew 10:28 informs us that we have much more to fear, *"And fear not them which kill the body, but are not able to kill the soul: but rather fear him which is able to destroy both soul and body in hell."*

Jonah would have done well to remember the words of Joshua: *"Now therefore fear the LORD, and serve him in sincerity and in truth: and put away the gods which your fathers served on the other side of the flood, and in Egypt; and serve ye the LORD"* (Joshua 24:14).

## B. A Fatal Conclusion

Jonah knew that the only hope these men had of saving their lives was to take his. *"And he said unto them, Take me up, and cast me forth into the sea; so shall the sea be calm unto you: for I know that for my sake this great tempest is upon you"* (Jonah 1:12).

No one ever plans on sin coming to such a tragic ending. No one plans at the wedding altar for their marriage to end in divorce. No one who holds their infant child plans on him running away from home. No one who takes a first drink plans on killing someone on a lonely highway as a drunk driver. Nor does anyone who takes a few steps away from God's will plan on being responsible for someone else's life!

But *"The soul that sinneth, it shall die"* (Ezekiel 18:20). *"Be not deceived; God is not mocked: for whatsoever a man soweth, that shall he also reap. For he that soweth to his flesh shall of the flesh reap corruption; but he that soweth to the Spirit shall of the Spirit reap life everlasting"* (Galatians 6:7–8). *"…There is a sin unto death…"* (1 John 5:16).

## II. A Sacrificial Reconciliation

Again, in verse sixteen, these men are offering up a sacrifice to the Lord. When these men left port a few hours earlier, I don't think they were planning on conducting "a chapel on the waves."

### A. The Effort of Man

These men had no doubt been in storms before. There was a typical routine that was followed in these situations. Their emergency plan is seen in verse thirteen: *"Nevertheless the men rowed hard to bring it to the land; but they could not: for the sea wrought, and was tempestuous against them."* They had already appealed to their gods and had dumped everything they owned overboard in verse five: *"Then the mariners were afraid, and cried every man unto his god, and cast forth the wares that were in the ship into the sea, to lighten it of them....*"

The true God is often man's last resort. We try everything we can to rid ourselves of the guilt of sin, but to no avail. We try religion (their gods), we try reformation (cast forth the wares), we try good works (the men rowed hard), but nothing atones for sin until we go to God. *"Where is boasting then? It is excluded. By what law? of works? Nay: but by the law of faith. Therefore we conclude that a man is justified by faith without the deeds of the law"* (Romans 3:27–28). We see in Ephesians that man's best effort cannot save him. *"For by grace are ye saved through faith; and that not of yourselves: it is the gift of God: Not of works, lest any man should boast"* (Ephesians 2:8–9).

Just as the unsaved, God's people cannot get through the storms of life on their own. *"Not that we are sufficient of ourselves to think any thing as of ourselves; but our sufficiency is of God"* (2 Corinthians 3:5). *"I am the vine, ye are the branches: He that abideth in me, and I in him, the same bringeth forth much fruit: for without me ye can do nothing"* (John 15:5). God didn't say we are or could do something or a little bit without Him. He said, "You are nothing without Me!"

## B. The Elusiveness of Mercy

Upon reaching the conclusion that they could do nothing, these mariners now cast themselves at the mercy of God. Verse fourteen says, *"Wherefore they cried unto the LORD, and said, We beseech thee, O LORD, we beseech thee, let us not perish for this man's life, and lay not upon us innocent blood: for thou, O LORD, hast done as it pleased thee."*

God's mercy doesn't come on our terms. God does not negotiate His grace. There is only one way to Heaven and that is through Jesus Christ. John 14:6 says, *"…I am the way, the truth, and the life: no man cometh unto the Father, but by me."*

The formula for revival is simple and straightforward: *"If my people, which are called by my name, shall humble themselves, and pray, and seek my face, and turn from their wicked ways; then will I hear from heaven, and will forgive their sin, and will heal their land"* (2 Chronicles 7:14).

Isaiah 55:6–7 is applicable to all: *"Seek ye the LORD while he may be found, call ye upon him while he is near: Let the wicked forsake his way, and the unrighteous man his thoughts: and let him return unto the LORD, and he will have mercy upon him; and to our God, for he will abundantly pardon."*

# III. A Surrendered Resolve

In verse sixteen, we read that these men, in the middle of a storm, made vows! The God who is told "No" in church is often told "Yes" in crisis.

## A. A Serious Moment

*"So they took up Jonah, and cast him forth into the sea: and the sea ceased from her raging."*—JONAH 1:15

Taking the life of another is a serious crime. Genesis 9:6 says, *"Whoso sheddeth man's blood, by man shall his blood be shed: for in the image of God made he man."* These men realized that if they were mistaking God's command here, they would be guilty of murder.

The Christian life is not a game. Walking an aisle and making decisions is an important matter. *"When thou vowest a vow unto God, defer not to pay it; for he hath no pleasure in fools: pay that which thou hast vowed. Better is it that thou shouldest not vow, than that thou shouldest vow and not pay"* (Ecclesiastes 5:4–5).

Decisions must be based on God's Word and then once those decisions are made, they are to be kept. *"For it had been better for them not to have known the way of righteousness, than, after they have known it, to turn from the holy commandment delivered unto them"* (2 Peter 2:21).

### B. A Supernatural Miracle

Do you suppose that these men watched as they threw Jonah over the edge of that boat? Perhaps they hoped he was a good swimmer and could survive until God appeased the storm. On the other hand, they no doubt had seen men go overboard before, only to quickly drown under the waves of the fierce sea.

*"Now the LORD had prepared a great fish to swallow up Jonah…"* (Jonah 1:17). Have you ever been to a place like Sea World where you were sitting patiently on some metal seats chatting with your friends waiting for the aquatic show to begin, when all of the sudden out of the water jumps this giant killer whale? The sight of that monstrous mammal and the thunderous splash of sea water that follows is impressive to say the least. That's the picture that comes to mind here as I read this passage. If these men didn't believe that God was behind the storm, they had to believe that God was controlling that whale!

No wonder we read that in verse sixteen: *"Then the men feared the LORD exceedingly, and offered a sacrifice unto the LORD, and made vows."* But do we really have to wait for a storm and a fish to obey God? Romans 2:4 asks, *"Or despisest thou the riches of his goodness and forbearance and longsuffering; not knowing that the goodness of God leadeth thee to repentance?"*

It may not seem as critical, but it surely is easier to make decisions for God on dry land!

SECTION TWO

# A Second Chance

# The Plan of Jehovah

## Key Verse

*"Now the LORD had prepared a great fish to swallow up Jonah. And Jonah was in the belly of the fish three days and three nights."*—JONAH 1:17

## Overview

Nothing takes God by surprise—not even our disobedience. And in spite of ourselves, God has a plan for our lives. *"A man's heart deviseth his way: but the LORD directeth his steps"* (Proverbs 16:9). *"There are many devices in a man's heart; nevertheless the counsel of the LORD, that shall stand"* (Proverbs 19:21).

## Lesson Theme

Man sees life from the playing field, but God sees life from the blimp. God's thoughts are higher than ours and His ways are better than ours. Our goal ought to be to *"...prove what is that good, and acceptable, and perfect, will of God"* (Romans 12:2).

## Lesson Objectives

- To reinforce in the student's mind that God does not abandon His plan for our lives just because we resist His will and go our own way.

- To encourage the student to believe that God does give second chances when we mess up our lives.
- To help the student forget what is behind and press toward that which is ahead in our lives.
- To establish the fact that God's plan does not simply affect us, but has an impact on all of God's work as a whole.

## Teaching Outline

I. A Divine Preparation
  A. God's Plan Is Pre-determined
  B. God's Plan Is Predominant

II. A Dutiful Pliability
  A. An Omnipotent Coincidence
  B. An Obedient Creation

III. A Distinct Prophecy
  A. An Ironic Typology
  B. An Illuminating Timetable

# The Plan of Jehovah

## Text

*"Now the* LORD *had prepared a great fish to swallow up Jonah. And Jonah was in the belly of the fish three days and three nights."*—JONAH 1:17

How thankful we should be for Divine intervention. None of us would be saved if God had not stepped into our lives and brought us under conviction and then to Himself. Jeremiah 31:3 states, *"The* LORD *hath appeared of old unto me, saying, Yea, I have loved thee with an everlasting love: therefore with lovingkindness have I drawn thee."* Jesus emphasized this point in John 6:44 when He said, *"No man can come to me, except the Father which hath sent me draw him…."*

In the book of Proverbs the "simple man" is described as one who is often caught in the middle—reacting to what is going on around him without any direction for his life. The word *simple* in Proverbs means "space" or "room." That is, there is still room for him to decide and as a result he is easily influenced.

God still loves this simple man and has a plan for his life. Listen to the words of the psalmist in Psalm 116:6–9, *"The LORD preserveth the simple: I was brought low, and he helped me. Return unto thy rest, O my soul; for the LORD hath dealt bountifully with thee. For thou hast delivered my soul from death, mine eyes from tears, and my feet from falling. I will walk before the LORD in the land of the living."*

Jonah was a "simple" man who was in desperate need of a second chance. And our great God gave him one!

# I. A Divine Preparation

*"Now the LORD had prepared a great fish to swallow up Jonah…."*
—JONAH 1:17

It's a good thing that God is always one step ahead of us. The psalmist states in Psalm 40:17, *"But I am poor and needy; yet the Lord thinketh upon me: thou art my help and my deliverer; make no tarrying, O my God."* I love the sovereignty of God that is seen in Isaiah 65:24: *"And it shall come to pass, that before they call, I will answer; and while they are yet speaking, I will hear."*

## A. God's Plan Is Pre-determined

God knew who we were, what we were going to look like, and what He wanted from our lives before we were born—and He had it all written down! *"For thou hast possessed my reins: thou hast covered me in my mother's womb. I will praise thee; for I am fearfully and wonderfully made: marvellous are thy works; and that my soul knoweth right well. My substance was not hid from thee, when I was made in secret, and curiously wrought in the lowest parts of the earth. Thine eyes did see my substance, yet being unperfect; and in thy book all my members were written, which in continuance were fashioned, when as yet there was none of them. How precious also are thy thoughts unto me, O God! how great is the sum of them!"* (Psalm 139:13–17).

We may not always see God's work or sense His presence in our lives, but that does not mean He has abandoned us. *"Behold, I go forward, but he is not there; and backward, but I cannot perceive him: On the left hand, where he doth work, but I cannot behold him: he hideth himself on the right hand, that I cannot see him: But he knoweth the way that I take: when he hath tried me, I shall come forth as gold"* (Job 23:8–10).

### B. God's Plan Is Predominant

Why is it that we think our plans are better than God's? Has He ever been unfaithful? Has He ever failed to come through on His promises? Has He ever forsaken us? *"The steps of a good man are ordered by the LORD: and he delighteth in his way. Though he fall, he shall not be utterly cast down: for the LORD upholdeth him with his hand. I have been young, and now am old; yet have I not seen the righteous forsaken, nor his seed begging bread"* (Psalm 37:23–25).

God's desire is that, *"...in all things he might have the preeminence"* (Colossians 1:18). And when God is first—we have nothing to worry about. *"But seek ye first the kingdom of God, and his righteousness; and all these things shall be added unto you"* (Matthew 6:33).

# II. A Dutiful Pliability

One of the great abilities God is looking for is pliability. Now, so far, we haven't seen too much of this characteristic in the life of Jonah. But we are about to see a great example of pliability—in a fish! I don't suppose this fish had a desire on his own to swim near the surface of the sea while lightening bolts were flashing all around him. A much safer place in the middle of a storm for a fish would be several feet under water! But we must remember that *"...all are thy servants"* (Psalm 119:91).

## A. An Omnipotent Coincidence

To man it might appear that it is merely coincidence that a fish just so happened to be swimming near this boat at the very time Jonah was tossed overboard. But there are no coincidences with God. Job 14:16 says, *"For now thou numberest my steps: dost thou not watch over my sin?"* *"Doth not he see my ways, and count all my steps?"* (Job 31:4).

Whether it was a boy with a sling or a boy with a lunch—there are no coincidences. They are all part of God's perfect and wonderful plan.

## B. An Obedient Creation

We can learn a lot from God's creation. *"But ask now the beasts, and they shall teach thee; and the fowls of the air, and they shall tell thee: Or speak to the earth, and it shall teach thee: and the fishes of the sea shall declare unto thee. Who knoweth not in all these that the hand of the LORD hath wrought this? In whose hand is the soul of every living thing, and the breath of all mankind"* (Job 12:7–10).

God marvels that so much of His creation is obedient to His will, while man struggles with His will. *"Yea, the stork in the heaven knoweth her appointed times; and the turtle and the crane and the swallow observe the time of their coming; but my people know not the judgment of the* LORD" (Jeremiah 8:7).

It's easy to talk about obedience, but God is looking for more than words. Mark Twain encountered a ruthless businessman from Boston during his travels who boasted that nobody ever got in his way once he determined to do something. He said, "Before I die I mean to take a pilgrimage to the Holy Land. I'm gonna climb Mount Sinai. And when I'm up there I'm gonna read the Ten Commandments aloud at the top of my voice!" Unimpressed, Twain responded, "I got a better idea. Stay in Boston and keep 'em."

# III. A Distinct Prophecy

*"...And Jonah was in the belly of the fish three days and three nights"* (Jonah 1:17). By now I hope you realize that nothing happens or is recorded in God's Word by accident. The fact that Jonah was swallowed by a whale is indeed fascinating, but there is more to the story than that.

## A. *An Ironic Typology*

The Old Testament is filled with "types" or pictures that are used to describe and foretell future truth. The brazen serpent in Exodus is a picture of Christ being lifted up on a cross according to John 3. The Paschal Lamb of the Old Testament is a wonderful picture of the Lamb of God as recognized by John the Baptist in John 1:29.

Jesus points to this picture of Jonah in the whale in Matthew 12:40: *"For as Jonas was three days and three nights in the whale's belly; so shall the Son of man be three days and three nights in the heart of the earth."*

Ironically, God takes the results of Jonah's disobedience to typify the obedience of His Son Jesus Christ. *"And being found in fashion as a man, he humbled himself, and became obedient unto death, even the death of the cross"* (Philippians 2:8).

### B.  An Illuminating Timetable

The three days and three nights here in the book of Jonah may seem insignificant, but it is indeed prophetic of the time that Jesus Christ would spend in the tomb. Jesus said in Mark 10:33–34, *"...Behold, we go up to Jerusalem; and the Son of man shall be delivered unto the chief priests, and unto the scribes; and they shall condemn him to death, and shall deliver him to the Gentiles: And they shall mock him, and shall scourge him, and shall spit upon him, and shall kill him: and the third day he shall rise again."*

Satan thought he had defeated Jonah and Jesus. But after three days of celebrating, the devil's victory parade turned into defeat on both occasions!

If you are living a defeated life today—remember, God gives second chances. Tomorrow is a clean slate. *"Now unto him that is able to keep you from falling, and to present you faultless before the presence of his glory with exceeding joy"* (Jude 24).

# The Prayer of Jonah

## Key Verses

*"Then Jonah prayed unto the LORD his God out of the fish's belly, And said, I cried by reason of mine affliction unto the LORD, and he heard me; out of the belly of hell cried I, and thou heardest my voice. For thou hadst cast me into the deep, in the midst of the seas; and the floods compassed me about: all thy billows and thy waves passed over me. Then I said, I am cast out of thy sight; yet I will look again toward thy holy temple. The waters compassed me about, even to the soul: the depth closed me round about, the weeds were wrapped about my head. I went down to the bottoms of the mountains; the earth with her bars was about me for ever: yet hast thou brought up my life from corruption, O LORD my God. When my soul fainted within me I remembered the LORD: and my prayer came in unto thee, into thine holy temple. They that observe lying vanities forsake their own mercy. But I will sacrifice unto thee with the voice of thanksgiving; I will pay that that I have vowed. Salvation is of the LORD."*—JONAH 2:1–9

## Overview

Prayer is not the Christian's good luck charm. It is important that God's people be faithful in good times as well as in bad. When we turn a deaf ear to God in the good times, we should not be surprised when He turns a deaf ear to us in the bad times. *"Then shall they call upon me, but I will not answer; they shall seek me early, but they shall not find me: For that they hated knowledge, and did not choose the fear of the LORD"* (Proverbs 1:28–29).

## Lesson Theme

Obedience is a twenty-four/seven project! God is pleased with consistent faithfulness, not simply when we are in a bind. *"Therefore, my beloved brethren, be ye stedfast, unmoveable, always abounding in the work of the Lord, forasmuch as ye know that your labour is not in vain in the Lord"* (1 Corinthians 15:58).

## Lesson Objectives

- To build a consistent relationship with God in the student's life, rather than simply trusting Him in times of difficulty.
- To help the student understand that "crisis Christianity" usually doesn't last past the crisis.
- To encourage the student to make vows and then keep them for the glory of God.

## Teaching Outline

I. Affliction-Driven Principles
   A. A Motivated Rebel
   B. A Miserable Reward

II. Adversity-Driven Prayers
   A. Cries from a Foxhole
   B. Concern from a Father

III. Avoidance-Driven Promises
   A. A Careful Voice
   B. A Continued Vow
   C. A Certain Victory

# The Prayer of Jonah

## Text

*"Then Jonah prayed unto the* LORD *his God out of the fish's belly. And said, I cried by reason of mine affliction unto the* LORD*, and he heard me; out of the belly of hell cried I, and thou heardest my voice. For thou hadst cast me into the deep, in the midst of the seas; and the floods compassed me about: all thy billows and thy waves passed over me. Then I said, I am cast out of thy sight; yet I will look again toward thy holy temple. The waters compassed me about, even to the soul: the depth closed me round about, the weeds were wrapped about my head. I went down to the bottoms of the mountains; the earth with her bars was about me for ever: yet hast thou brought up my life from corruption, O* LORD *my God. When my soul fainted within me I remembered the* LORD*: and my prayer came in unto thee, into thine holy temple. They that observe lying vanities forsake their own mercy. But I will sacrifice unto*

*thee with the voice of thanksgiving; I will pay that that I have vowed. Salvation is of the LORD."*—JONAH 2:1–9

It might appear that we are being a little hard on Jonah in this lesson. However, by the time we get to Jonah chapter four, I think that all will agree that his sudden spirituality in chapter two is flawed to say the least.

*"Then Jonah prayed unto the LORD his God out of the fish's belly"* (Jonah 2:1). Jonah didn't pray about obeying God, or buying a ticket to Tarshish, or about sleeping during the storm. But now, when his life is hanging in the balance, he suddenly gets serious enough to pray about his circumstance.

As a boy, I hated going to the dentist. Due to "soft" teeth, I always had multiple cavities that needed to be drilled out and then filled. In those days, they didn't use pain killers of any kind and dentists were trained in the art of torture!

I remember one day sitting in the dentist's chair waiting for him to start poking around in my mouth. My eyes were already watering just thinking about the pain I was about to endure. As a small boy, I began to pray. I said, "Dear Lord, if you will let me get out of this chair without a single cavity, just this once—I will never sin again!" I was as sincere as I could be and even though I was not saved, I had never been more honest in my life.

To my surprise, the dentist could not find a single cavity in my mouth. He was as shocked as I was as he took that little napkin from around my neck and told me I could go. As I stood to my feet, God reminded me of my promise. I knew that I could never keep what I had vowed and it served as a lesson in my life to be careful about what I prayed during times of adversity.

# I. Affliction-Driven Principles

*"...I cried by reason of mine affliction unto the* Lord*...."*
—Jonah 2:2

When is the last time you prayed? Does it take some crisis for you to find a place on your knees? Oh sure, we need to pray in times of affliction, but God wants our worship all of the time.

Daniel was a consistent man of God. As a result, his enemies conspired against him and got the king to sign a petition making it illegal to pray. In Daniel 6:10, it says, *"Now when Daniel knew that the writing was signed, he went into his house; and his windows being open in his chamber toward Jerusalem, he kneeled upon his knees three times a day, and prayed, and gave thanks before his God, **as he did aforetime**."* Yes, he needed to pray during this affliction, but nothing changed when the affliction came. He had been praying long before the trial.

## A. A Motivated Rebel

*"And said, I cried by reason of mine affliction unto the* Lord, *and he heard me; out of the belly of hell cried I, and thou heardest my voice"* (Jonah 2:2). Affliction is a powerful motivator!

Like Jonah, Samson had run a course of disobedience. Warning after warning had gone unheeded. Close call after close call had been casually cast aside. Now with his eyes put out and the crowd jeering him, he says, *"...O Lord* God, *remember me, I pray thee, and strengthen me, I pray thee, only this once, O God, that I may be at once avenged of the Philistines for my two eyes"* (Judges 16:28).

### B. A Miserable Reward

There is pleasure in sin for a season (Hebrews 11:25). *"Folly is joy to him that is destitute of wisdom: but a man of understanding walketh uprightly"* (Proverbs 15:21). The path of disobedience may be smooth sailing for a while, but the season of sin is always short.

Whatever price Jonah was unwilling to pay when God asked him to preach to Nineveh now seems pretty meager in comparison to the cost of his disobedience!

*"For thou hadst cast me into the deep, in the midst of the seas; and the floods compassed me about: all thy billows and thy waves passed over me. Then I said, I am cast out of thy sight; yet I will look again toward thy holy temple. The waters compassed me about, even to the soul: the depth closed me round about, the weeds were wrapped about my head. I went down to the bottoms of the mountains; the earth with her bars was about me for ever: yet hast thou brought up my life from corruption, O LORD my God."*
—JONAH 2:3–6

*"As righteousness tendeth to life; so he that pursueth evil pursueth it to his own death."*—PROVERBS 11:19

*"Dead flies cause the ointment of the apothecary to send forth a stinking savour: so doth a little folly him that is in reputation for wisdom and honour."*
—ECCLESIASTES 10:1

## II. Adversity-Driven Prayers

*"When my soul fainted within me I remembered the LORD: and my prayer came in unto thee, into thine holy temple."*
—JONAH 2:7

## A. Cries from a Foxhole

If there ever was a "foxhole" prayer—this was it! David prayed a similar prayer in Psalm 69:1–5: "*Save me, O God for the waters are come in unto my soul. I sink in deep mire, where there is no standing: I am come into deep waters, where the floods overflow me. I am weary of my crying: my throat is dried: mine eyes fail while I wait for my God. They that hate me without a cause are more than the hairs of mine head: they that would destroy me, being mine enemies wrongfully, are mighty: then I restored that which I took not away. O God, thou knowest my foolishness; and my sins are not hid from thee.*"

## B. Concern from a Father

"*When my soul fainted within me I remembered the* Lord: *and my prayer came in unto thee, into thine holy temple*" (Jonah 2:7). The father of a prodigal is disappointed to say the least, but he always waits for his son to return home!

God sometimes puts us in the dark to prove to us that He is the Light! Vance Havner said, "Sometimes your medicine bottle has on it: 'Shake well before using.' That is what God has to do with some of His people. He has to shake them well before they are ever usable."

"*Who is a God like unto thee, that pardoneth iniquity, and passeth by the transgression of the remnant of his heritage? he retaineth not his anger for ever, because he delighteth in mercy*" (Micah 7:18). "*I, even I, am he that blotteth out thy transgressions for mine own sake, and will not remember thy sins*" (Isaiah 43:25).

God never tires of true repentance. "*The sacrifices of God are a broken spirit: a broken and a contrite heart, O God, thou wilt not despise*" (Psalm 51:17).

# III. Avoidance-Driven Promises

*"...I will pay that that I have vowed..."* (Jonah 2:9). When we make promises to God, we must make sure that we have every intent to keep them. Promises made to simply escape punishment are not pleasing to the Lord.

### A. A Careful Voice

*"But I will sacrifice unto thee with the voice of thanksgiving...."*
—JONAH 2:9

Do you think that Jonah was really thankful? He wasn't thankful in chapter one and he won't be thankful in chapter four, so what is motivating this sudden gratefulness?

James reminds us to, *"...let your yea be yea; and your nay, nay; lest ye fall into condemnation"* (James 5:12). We must be careful with the words we speak and promises we make.

### B. A Continued Vow

*"...I will pay that that I have vowed..."* (Jonah 2:9). God takes our vows seriously.

*"If a man vow a vow unto the LORD, or swear an oath to bind his soul with a bond; he shall not break his word, he shall do according to all that proceedeth out of his mouth"* (Numbers 30:2). *"When thou shalt vow a vow unto the LORD thy God, thou shalt not slack to pay it: for the LORD thy God will surely require it of thee; and it would be sin in thee"* (Deuteronomy 23:21).

I believe that we would see revival in our churches if every member would make just one decision. I don't know if we would ever need to make another decision after this one. Just one more decision would change everything! Do you know what that decision would be? To keep every decision we have already made!

## C. A Certain Victory

"...*Salvation is of the* LORD" (Jonah 2:9). This may be the only really true phrase uttered in this entire prayer. If victory comes, it can come no other way but through the Lord.

*"But the salvation of the righteous is of the* LORD: *he is their strength in the time of trouble."*—PSALM 37:39

*"Some trust in chariots, and some in horses: but we will remember the name of the* LORD *our God."*—PSALM 20:7

No matter how dark the situation—there is always hope in God. He is the master of snatching victory from the jaws of defeat. *"O death, where is thy sting? O grave, where is thy victory? The sting of death is sin; and the strength of sin is the law. But thanks be to God, which giveth us the victory through our Lord Jesus Christ"* (1 Corinthians 15:55–57).

Don't wait for the foxhole to start building your relationship with God. You'll have a lot more confidence in your God, if you obey Him before the bullets start flying! The storm in Paul's life as recorded in Acts 27 was just as severe as the one Jonah faced here, but while Jonah fears for his life, Paul is at perfect peace in the will of God. And you can be too!

A short prayer can reach God if you don't live too far away!

# The Proceeding of the Journey

## Key Verses

*"And the* LORD *spake unto the fish, and it vomited out Jonah upon the dry land. And the word of the* LORD *came unto Jonah the second time, saying, Arise, go unto Nineveh, that great city, and preach unto it the preaching that I bid thee."*
—JONAH 2:10–3:2

## Overview

Our obstinate will does not change God's omniscient will! We cannot understand everything in God's plan for our lives, but God will not change His will to accommodate our wishes. Since His plan is perfect, there is never any reason to change it.

## Lesson Theme

We should obey God the first time He speaks, because our delay will not change His direction. God knows that we will only have joy in life if we are in the center of His will, and He jealously works in our lives to bring us to that place.

## Lesson Objectives

- To help the student realize that our decisions, both good and bad, determine what our destiny will be.

- To enable the student to get back up after failure.
- To encourage the student to realize that God is a God of second chances, and victory in our lives is just an obedient step away.
- To challenge the student to obey God the first time He speaks, realizing that God will not change His mind about His plan for our lives simply because we do not want to obey.

## Teaching Outline

    I.  A Sick Constitution
       A.  Class Dismissed
       B.  Classic Delivery

    II.  A Second Chance
       A.  An Attentive Lord
       B.  An Amazing Longsuffering

    III.  A Same Communication
       A.  Man Can Abuse God's Patience
       B.  Man Cannot Alter God's Plan

# The Proceeding of the Journey

## Text

*"And the LORD spake unto the fish, and it vomited out Jonah upon the dry land. And the word of the LORD came unto Jonah the second time, saying, Arise, go unto Nineveh, that great city, and preach unto it the preaching that I bid thee."*
—JONAH 2:10–3:2

If this story were put in drama form, there would be a number of scene changes. Beginning here with verse ten of chapter two is another one of those transitions in the story. *"And the LORD spake unto the fish."* It's a good thing this fish was listening to God, or none of this could have taken place. Of course by now, this fish is probably sick of Jonah anyway! Bad preachers can cause indigestion for anyone.

On a more serious note, I'm glad that God is patient. I'm glad He doesn't give up when we do. None of us would have wasted any more time with Jonah. But God was not just interested in Nineveh—He was interested in Jonah. God could have used anybody, but He chose to use Jonah.

God is intensely interested in this world being saved, and He could use any number of ways to get the job done. But He has chosen to use us! From our perspective, this is not a very wise choice, but think about what Paul says in 1 Corinthians 1:26–29, *"For ye see your calling, brethren, how that not many wise men after the flesh, not many mighty, not many noble, are called: But God hath chosen the foolish things of the world to confound the wise: and God hath chosen the weak things of the world to confound the things which are mighty; And base things of the world, and things which are despised, hath God chosen, yea, and things which are not, to bring to nought things that are: That no flesh should glory in his presence."*

God wants to use us in a way that is much bigger than ourselves, but He also wants to be "big" in our lives during the process.

# I.  A Sick Constitution

*"And the LORD spake unto the fish, and it vomited out Jonah upon the dry land"* (Jonah 2:10). Don't you love the picture these words paint in your mind? I have often hoped that there would be video rooms in Heaven where we can go watch replays of these events. This is one I would love to see!

Have you ever used the phrase "You make me sick"? God literally made this fish sick. I believe it was a quick exit, as well, for this fish was no doubt tired of housing this backslidden preacher. All God had to do was give the word, and Jonah was back on dry land. *"For he spake, and it was done; he commanded, and it stood fast"* (Psalm 33:9).

God spoke and the world was created. God spoke, and Jesus arose from the grave. God will one day speak, and we will be taken up to glory! All it takes is a word from God!

## A.  Class Dismissed

The curriculum has been taught, the final exam given, and Jonah is ready to graduate from "Seaweed Seminary." The sooner we learn to obey, the sooner we can proceed in the journey of God's perfect will.

I like the words to the following children's song: "Obedience is the very best way to show that you believe. Doing exactly what the Lord commands, doing it happily. Action is the key—do it immediately. Joy you will receive. Obedience is the very best way to show that you believe."

*"If ye love me, keep my commandments."*—JOHN 14:15

*"Ye are my friends, if ye do whatsoever I command you."*—JOHN 15:14

## B.  Classic Delivery

It is interesting to see in verse ten that Jonah was vomited onto *dry land*. What an immediate contrast to where he had spent the last three days and nights. From floods, billows, and waves in verse three and waters and weeds in verse five, Jonah is suddenly standing on *dry land*! For the past seventy-two hours he has longed for this moment. What a difference obedience makes!

*"I waited patiently for the LORD; and he inclined unto me, and heard my cry. He brought me up also out of an horrible pit, out of the miry clay, and set my feet upon a rock, and established my goings"* (Psalm 40:1–2). *"Therefore if any man be in Christ, he is a new creature:*

*old things are passed away; behold, all things are become new"* (2 Corinthians 5:17). If you have never experienced the change that comes with salvation, *"now is the day of salvation!"*

As a Christian, the blessings will begin in your life with the next step of obedience. *"But whoso looketh into the perfect law of liberty, and continueth therein, he being not a forgetful hearer, but a doer of the work, this man shall be blessed in his deed"* (James 1:25).

# II.  A Second Chance

*"And the word of the LORD came unto Jonah the second time, saying,"*—JONAH 3:1

Every one of us ought to thank God daily that He *"is merciful and gracious, slow to anger, and plenteous in mercy"* (Psalm 103:8).

## A.  An Attentive Lord

Aren't you glad that when you call on God you never get voicemail? You never get an answering machine or an "unable to deliver" notification. *"The eyes of the LORD are upon the righteous, and his ears are open unto their cry"* (Psalm 34:15).

In the life of Christ, we see His attentiveness to the needs of people from all walks of life. The woman at the well, the man in a tree, the blind beggar by the roadside, the widow with two mites, and the thief on the cross are all examples of His all-seeing eye and always-caring heart.

While we often focus on the fact that God sees us when we sin, it is a great truth to know that God also sees us when we are obedient. Men may overlook your faithfulness, but God never does. *"For God is not unrighteous to forget your work and labour of love, which ye have shewed toward his name, in that ye have ministered to the saints, and do minister"* (Hebrews 6:10).

Did you know that God has His own "palm pilot" and your name is on it? *"Can a woman forget her sucking child, that she should not have compassion on the son of her womb? yea, they may forget, yet will I not forget thee. Behold, I have graven thee upon the palms of my hands"* (Isaiah 49:15–16).

## B. An Amazing Longsuffering

How would we have dealt with Jonah had he defied our orders and ignored our message? Probably written him off for good! But not God—for *"…the word of the LORD came unto Jonah the **second** time…"* (Jonah 3:1).

When Peter came to the Lord in Matthew 18, he asked Him in verse twenty-one, *"…Lord, how oft shall my brother sin against me, and I forgive him? till seven times? Jesus saith unto him, I say not unto thee, Until seven times: but, Until seventy times seven."*

I wonder how different our relationships would be at home, at work, and at church if we practiced the longsuffering of the Lord? So often, the Spirit of God is quenched because of bitter and unforgiving spirits.

*"And grieve not the holy Spirit of God, whereby ye are sealed unto the day of redemption. Let all bitterness, and wrath, and anger, and clamour, and evil speaking, be put away from you, with all malice: And be ye kind one to*

*another, tenderhearted, forgiving one another, even as God for Christ's sake hath forgiven you."*—EPHESIANS 4:30–32

If God, in His patience and longsuffering, has forgiven me of every sin, there is no one I cannot forgive with His help. George Herbert said, "He who cannot forgive others breaks the bridge over which he must pass himself." Benjamin Franklin stated, "Doing an injury puts you below your enemy; revenging makes you but even with him; forgiving sets you above him."

## III. A Same Communication

In chapter one and verse two, God commanded Jonah, *"Arise, go to Nineveh, that great city, and cry against it…."* Now in chapter three and verse two, He says, *"Arise, go unto Nineveh, that great city, and preach unto it the preaching that I bid thee."* The assignment has not changed! Your obstinate will does not change God's omniscient will!

### A. Man Can Abuse God's Patience

You may be thinking that since God is a patient God, you have plenty of time to serve Him but consider the words of Ecclesiastes 8:11, *"Because sentence against an evil work is not executed speedily, therefore the heart of the sons of men is fully set in them to do evil."*

Be careful! God warns us in Proverbs 29:1 that *"He, that being often reproved hardeneth his neck, shall suddenly be destroyed, and that without remedy."* Paul said, *"I do not frustrate the grace of God…"* (Galatians 2:21). God was patient with the people of Noah's day in spite of their wickedness, but His patience eventually ran out. *"…My spirit shall not always strive with man, for that he also is flesh: yet his days shall be an hundred and twenty years"* (Genesis 6:3).

Since you don't know where the "line" of God's patience is, it doesn't make much sense to keep walking in that direction. The old hymn-writer put it this way: "Have you counted the cost if your soul should be lost? Though you gain the whole world for your own. Even now it may be that the line you have crossed. Have you counted? Have you counted the cost?"

### B. Man Cannot Alter God's Plan

Man cannot alter God's plan and why would he want to, when His plan is perfect? How are you going to improve on perfect? We spend all of our energy trying to devise a plan that is better than God's, only to realize in the end that His plan was impeccable.

The captain of a ship looked out into the distance across the waters and saw a light directly in the path of his ship. He commanded his signalman to send a message, "Alter your course ten degrees north." A few moments later, a reply was received, "Alter *your* course ten degrees south." The captain was outraged. His message had been ignored. He sent a second message, "Alter your course ten degrees north—I am a Captain!" Soon a message was received, "Alter *your* course ten degrees south—I am Seaman, First-class Jones." The captain could not believe it. He sent a third message knowing the fear it would evoke, "Alter your course ten degrees north—I am a battleship!" A few moments passed and then a third message was received, "Alter *your* course ten degrees south—I am a lighthouse!"

Go ahead! Try to talk God into changing course! You'll find out in the end, that He isn't moving. *"For ever,*

*O LORD, thy word is settled in heaven*" (Psalm 119:89). Success never comes to the man who tries to change the Bible to fit his life. Success comes to the man who changes his life to fit the Bible.

# The Pronouncement of Judgment

## Key Verses

*"And the word of the LORD came unto Jonah the second time, saying, Arise, go unto Nineveh, that great city, and preach unto it the preaching that I bid thee. So Jonah arose, and went unto Nineveh, according to the word of the LORD. Now Nineveh was an exceeding great city of three days' journey. And Jonah began to enter into the city a day's journey, and he cried, and said, Yet forty days, and Nineveh shall be overthrown."*—JONAH 3:1–4

## Overview

When God gets an obedient servant, things can change very fast. God has the power to change lives, but it is often the backslidden condition of His people that holds back that power. *"Behold, the LORD's hand is not shortened, that it cannot save; neither his ear heavy, that it cannot hear: But your iniquities have separated between you and your God, and your sins have hid his face from you, that he will not hear"* (Isaiah 59:1–2).

## Lesson Theme

Phillips Brooks once said, "Preaching is truth and personality." In other words, you cannot separate the message from the messenger. They are intertwined and must work together. When God's Word is preached by God's man in God's way— watch out! Revival is on the way!

# Lesson Objectives

- To help the student understand that God has a solution to man's problem.
- To equip the student in bringing his behavior into sync with the message he believes.
- To challenge the student to simply use God's Word as a powerful weapon in the culture around him.
- To give the student an understanding of the resistance that comes when the Word of God is preached and lived.

# Teaching Outline

I. An Urgent Matter
    A. Preaching Is God's Answer
    B. Promptness Is God's Advice

II. A Useful Minister
    A. A Pliable Messenger
    B. A Plagiarized Message

III. An Unsavory Message
    A. The Wrath of God
    B. The Window of Grace

# The Pronouncement of Judgment

## Text

*"And the word of the LORD came unto Jonah the second time, saying, Arise, go unto Nineveh, that great city, and preach unto it the preaching that I bid thee. So Jonah arose, and went unto Nineveh, according to the word of the LORD. Now Nineveh was an exceeding great city of three days' journey. And Jonah began to enter into the city a day's journey, and he cried, and said, Yet forty days, and Nineveh shall be overthrown."*—JONAH 3:1–4

Finally, God had a willing and obedient servant. That's the good news. The bad news is: I wonder how many people died in this great city during the time that Jonah was messing around in his selfish disobedience?

We often marvel at testimonies of people who are saved out of terrible lifestyles of sin and disgrace. Certainly, we would not underestimate the power of such a testimony, but how many more people could have been reached had that person been saved at a young age and given his whole life to God?

One Sunday afternoon a pastor friend of D. L. Moody asked him how many were saved in his services that morning. Moody responded, "Two and a half." The friend said, "Oh, you mean you had two adults and one kid saved?" "No," said Moody. "We had two kids and one adult!" You see the adult had already wasted half of his life, so Moody only counted him as a half. The children, however, had their entire lives to live for God.

Regardless of when you got saved—make the rest of your life count for the Lord! Don't waste another moment of time that could be used in obedient service to the One who saved you.

# I.   An Urgent Matter

David said in 1 Samuel 21:8, "...*the king's business required haste.*" Paul challenges us in Romans 13:11–12, "*And that, knowing the time, that now it is high time to awake out of sleep: for now is our salvation nearer than when we believed. The night is far spent, the day is at hand: let us therefore cast off the works of darkness, and let us put on the armour of light.*" And again in Ephesians 5:16, "*Redeeming the time, because the days are evil.*" This is no time to be sitting on the sideline.

"*...The harvest truly is plenteous, but the labourers are few*" (Matthew 9:37). "*...Shall your brethren go to war, and shall ye sit here?*" (Numbers 32:6).

## A.  Preaching Is God's Answer

God's command to Jonah for Nineveh was to "*...preach unto it the preaching that I bid thee*" (Jonah 3:2). Man likes to think he has the answers and the methods to communicate those answers. But read what God says in 1 Corinthians 1:18–21, *"For the preaching of the cross is to them that perish foolishness; but unto us which are saved it is the power of God. For it is written, I will destroy the wisdom of the wise, and will bring to nothing the understanding of the prudent. Where is the wise? where is the scribe? where is the disputer of this world? hath not God made foolish the wisdom of this world? For after that in the wisdom of God the world by wisdom knew not God, it pleased God by the foolishness of preaching to save them that believe."*

God's Word is truth according to John 17:17 and in Titus 1:3, the Bible declares that God *"…hath in due times manifested his word through preaching…."* We have the answers to man's problems. It is time we start using God's Word. Charles Spurgeon stated, "It is blessed to eat into the very soul of the Bible until you come to talk in scriptural language and your spirit is flavored with the words of the Lord, so that your blood is bibline and the very essence of the Bible flows through you."

*"For as the rain cometh down, and the snow from heaven, and returneth not thither, but watereth the earth, and maketh it bring forth and bud, that it may give seed to the sower, and bread to the eater: So shall my word be that goeth forth out of my mouth: it shall not return unto me void, but it shall accomplish that which I please, and it shall prosper in the thing whereto I sent it."*—ISAIAH 55:10–11

## B. Promptness Is God's Advice

Jonah has learned the painful lesson of promptness! Nineveh was a city of three days' journey according to Jonah 3:3. In verse four it records for us that Jonah entered into the city *"a days' journey."* One could take this a couple of different ways. Perhaps when he landed on dry land he was a three days' journey from Nineveh, but because of his eagerness now to obey God, he made it there in a day. A more likely explanation is that Nineveh was a large city that took three days to travel across on foot. Jonah went a day's journey into the city and began to preach.

In either case, I think it is easy to see that Jonah was eager to deliver the message! God always speaks His message in the "present" tense. He never says, "Get saved tomorrow" or "Set your house in order someday." It is always: *"**To day** if ye will hear his voice, Harden not your heart"* (Psalm 95:7–8). *"Come **now**, and let us reason together, saith the LORD"* (Isaiah 1:18). *"Remember **now** thy Creator in the days of thy youth, while the evil days come not, nor the years draw nigh, when thou shalt say, I have no pleasure in them"* (Ecclesiastes 12:1). *"Behold, **now** is the accepted time; behold, **now** is the day of salvation"* (2 Corinthians 6:2).

If something is right to do—it's right to do it *today*. If it's worth doing—it's worth doing *now*!

## II. A Useful Minister

There is nothing more satisfying in life than being used of God in some way for His glory. After listing his resumé in Philippians 3:1–6, Paul writes, *"But what things were gain to me, those I counted loss for Christ. Yea doubtless, and I count all things but loss for the excellency of the knowledge of Christ Jesus my Lord: for whom I have suffered the loss of all things, and do count them but dung, that I may win Christ"* (verses 7–8).

Recently after preaching a funeral, the brother of the deceased came up to me at the graveside and asked if he could speak with me. Here was a man who was saved as a teenager and had been challenged many times to give his life for Christ. While he was not living in wicked sin, his life had been consumed with making a living. He had done a great job. I have been in his home—he has what the world would call a great portfolio. But he said to me there at the grave of his sister, "You know, I have a tendency to think that what I do is really important. As an engineer, people are constantly waiting on me to get my projects done so that the business can go forward. Without me, nothing can happen. But I have realized today, that it is you, as a preacher, that really has the important work. Your life counts for something bigger than anything in this world."

Only one life, 'twill soon be past—only what's done for Christ will last!

## A. A Pliable Messenger

Jonah was now ready to preach the message that God had given to him. Pliability may be the most important ability. When I was a young man, Dr. Joe Boyd said to me one day, "Son, you've got to learn to be ambidextrous." At the time, I had to go look that word up! Upon discovering the meaning, I knew what he meant. I was too set in my ways—I always wanted to do things my way. It was time that I learned to be flexible and willing to do things God's way.

"*I delight to do thy will, O my God: yea, thy law is within my heart*" (Psalm 40:8). Our great Example prayed, "*nevertheless not as I will, but as thou wilt*" (Matthew 26:39).

## B. A Plagiarized Message

I have a sermon that I call the "Scripture Sermon." In it, I use nothing but Bible verses from beginning to end. When people have commented on how God used that message in their lives, I have said, "I plagiarized the whole thing!" Here is one area where we won't get into trouble for "copying"!

*"And take...the sword of the Spirit, which is the word of God"* (Ephesians 6:17). *"And these words, which I command thee this day, shall be in thine heart: And thou shalt teach them diligently unto thy children, and shalt talk of them when thou sittest in thine house, and when thou walkest by the way, and when thou liest down, and when thou risest up. And thou shalt bind them for a sign upon thine hand, and they shall be as frontlets between thine eyes. And thou shalt write them upon the posts of thy house, and on thy gates"* (Deuteronomy 6:6-9).

Sometimes, a preacher will read his text from the Bible, set the Word of God aside (as if to get it out of the way) and then tell us what they think we need to hear. I always tell young men who are training to preach, "You would be better off to get what you are going to say out of the way and then pick up the Word of God and just read it!"

I remember preaching my first sermon in church to the teen Sunday school class. At the time, I was not called to preach, but I was definitely thinking about it and wondering if that was what God had for my life. The pastor of the church sent his wife down to the class to listen to my sermon (probably so he would know what he would need to straighten out later). Fortunately, after I finished, she came up and said, "John, that was a good sermon." Exhausted from the experience, I said, "I don't know where your husband gets all of his sermons!" She held out her Bible in front of her, looked at me, and said, "John, they're all in here." Wow! She was right. We don't have to come up with our own! God has a whole Book full of them waiting to be delivered!

# III. An Unsavory Message

"...Yet forty days, and Nineveh shall be overthrown" (Jonah 3:4). Not exactly the kind of sermon that wins friends, builds attendance, or stimulates a good love offering! In chapter one, God says of this city, that "...their wickedness is come up before me" (Jonah 1:2). Their reaction to this message was probably similar to those in Noah's day or Lot's day. But we only control our "actions" not other's "reactions."

Ezekiel had a similarly tough task: "But the house of Israel will not hearken unto thee; for they will not hearken unto me: for all the house of Israel are impudent and hardhearted. Behold, I have made thy face strong against their faces, and thy forehead strong against their foreheads. As an adamant harder than flint have I made thy forehead: fear them not, neither be dismayed at their looks, though they be a rebellious house" (Ezekiel 3:7–9).

## A. The Wrath of God

Judgment was about to fall. Jonah was commissioned to give these people one final warning. "He that believeth on the Son hath everlasting life: and he that believeth not the Son shall not see life; but the wrath of God abideth on him" (John 3:36). I wonder who we will meet today that needs a final warning?

God is a God of love, but He is also holy. Man thinks that God in His love will have pity and let him slip into

Heaven in spite of his sin. Listen to the warning given in Ezekiel 7:3–4: *"Now is the end come upon thee, and I will send mine anger upon thee, and will judge thee according to thy ways, and will recompense upon thee all thine abominations. And mine eye shall not spare thee, neither will I have pity: but I will recompense thy ways upon thee, and thine abominations shall be in the midst of thee: and ye shall know that I am the LORD."*

Yes, *"God is angry with the wicked every day"* (Psalm 7:11), and God has given us the responsibility of warning them.

### B. The Window of Grace

God could have destroyed Nineveh on the spot, but instead He gives them a window of forty days to repent. We do not know when Christ will return or how long we have to live, but the time we have to do business with God is a gift of His grace. That window may remain open for many years or it could close today.

*"Boast not thyself of to morrow; for thou knowest not what a day may bring forth."*—PROVERBS 27:1

Like the Apostle Paul, we need to recognize and respond in our lives to God's grace: *"But by the grace of God I am what I am: and his grace which was bestowed upon me was not in vain; but I laboured more abundantly than they all: yet not I, but the grace of God which was with me"* (1 Corinthians 15:10).

You are no doubt familiar with the little nursery rhyme:

> Humpty Dumpty sat on a wall;
> Humpty Dumpty had a great fall.

All the king's horses and all the king's men,
Could not put Humpty Dumpty back together again.

Someone has wisely written:

Jesus Christ came to our wall;
Jesus Christ died for our fall.
So that regardless of death and in spite of sin,
Through grace, He might put us together again.

# The Process of Justification

## Key Verses

*"So the people of Nineveh believed God, and proclaimed a fast, and put on sackcloth, from the greatest of them even to the least of them. For word came unto the king of Nineveh, and he arose from his throne, and he laid his robe from him, and covered him with sackcloth, and sat in ashes. And he caused it to be proclaimed and published through Nineveh by the decree of the king and his nobles, saying, Let neither man nor beast, herd nor flock, taste any thing: let them not feed, nor drink water: But let man and beast be covered with sackcloth, and cry mightily unto God: yea, let them turn every one from his evil way, and from the violence that is in their hands. Who can tell if God will turn and repent, and turn away from his fierce anger, that we perish not? And God saw their works, that they turned from their evil way; and God repented of the evil, that he had said that he would do unto them; and he did it not."*—JONAH 3:5–10

## Overview

God is always waiting for man to repent and is more than willing to cleanse and forgive when he does. *"Who is a God like unto thee, that pardoneth iniquity, and passeth by the transgression of the remnant of his heritage? he retaineth not his anger for ever, because he delighteth in mercy"* (Micah 7:18). God *delights* in mercy!

# Lesson Theme

Repentance is more than just a simple bed-time prayer of "please forgive me of all the wrong things I did today." We must seriously confess and forsake our wicked ways if we want God's blessing. *"He that covereth his sins shall not prosper: but whoso confesseth and forsaketh them shall have mercy"* (Proverbs 28:13).

# Lesson Objectives

- To show the student that God is a God of forgiveness and cleansing.
- To help the student understand what true repentance involves and the seriousness of confessing and forsaking sin.
- To focus the student on the blessing of forgiveness rather than on the curse of the past.
- To teach the student that every problem in life can be solved by turning to God in simple faith and trust in His Word.

# Teaching Outline

I. A Faith
   A. The Obligation of Faith
   B. The Object of Faith

II. A Fast
   A. The Ultimate Contrition
   B. A Universal Commitment

III. A Forsaking
   A. Repentance Involves a Change of Direction
   B. Repentance Involves a Change of Deeds

IV. A Forgiveness
   A. The Attention of God
   B. The Atonement of God

# The Process of Justification

## Text

*"So the people of Nineveh believed God, and proclaimed a fast, and put on sackcloth, from the greatest of them even to the least of them. For word came unto the king of Nineveh, and he arose from his throne, and he laid his robe from him, and covered him with sackcloth, and sat in ashes. And he caused it to be proclaimed and published through Nineveh by the decree of the king and his nobles, saying, Let neither man nor beast, herd nor flock, taste any thing: let them not feed, nor drink water: But let man and beast be covered with sackcloth, and cry mightily unto God: yea, let them turn every one from his evil way, and from the violence that is in their hands. Who can tell if God will turn and repent, and turn away from his fierce anger, that we perish not? And God saw their works, that they turned from their evil way; and God repented of the evil, that he had said that he would do unto them; and he did it not."*—JONAH 3:5–10

Job once asked, *"...How should man be just with God?"* (Job 9:2). Later in Job 25:4–6, he again ponders this dilemma: *"How then can man be justified with God? or how can he be clean that is born of a woman? Behold even to the moon, and it shineth not; yea, the stars are not pure in his sight. How much less man, that is a worm? and the son of man, which is a worm?"*

The Apostle Paul addresses this same question in a classic passage of Scripture found in Romans 7:14–25. While frustrated and depressed at the prospects of his sinful tendencies, he concludes with victory: *"For we know that the law is spiritual: but I am carnal, sold under sin. For that which I do I allow not: for what I would, that do I not; but what I hate, that do I. If then I do that which I would not, I consent unto the law that it is good. Now then it is no more I that do it, but sin that dwelleth in me. For I know that in me (that is, in my flesh,) dwelleth no good thing: for to will is present with me; but how to perform that which is good I find not. For the good that I would I do not: but the evil which I would not, that I do. Now if I do that I would not, it is no more I that do it, but sin that dwelleth in me. I find then a law, that, when I would do good, evil is present with me. For I delight in the law of God after the inward man: But I see another law in my members, warring against the law of my mind, and bringing me into captivity to the law of sin which is in my members. O wretched man that I am! who shall deliver me from the body of this death? I thank God through Jesus Christ our Lord. So then with the mind I myself serve the law of God; but with the flesh the law of sin."* He then adds in the next chapter in verse one, *"There is therefore now no condemnation to them which are in Christ Jesus, who walk not after the flesh, but after the Spirit."*

Our only hope of ever finding forgiveness from God is through the Person of the Lord Jesus Christ! Romans 5:1

says, *"Therefore being justified by faith, we have peace with God through our Lord Jesus Christ."*

# I.   A Faith

*"So the people of Nineveh believed God...."*—JONAH 3:5

Unlike religion, ceremony, good works, or some gimmick, faith is putting our trust in an Almighty God. Faith is believing in the invisible, looking for the incredible and seeing the impossible! And while faith is not always easy, without it, *"it is impossible to please him"* (Hebrews 11:6).

## A.   The Obligation of Faith

Faith in God is not an option—it is not one of many choices to find peace with God—it is an obligation. Salvation comes through no other means: *"For by grace are ye saved through faith..."* (Ephesians 2:8).

*"Where is boasting then? It is excluded. By what law? of works? Nay: but by the law of faith. Therefore we conclude that a man is justified by faith without the deeds of the law."*—ROMANS 3:27–28

The Apostle Paul probably attempted and accomplished more for God than any human being. His resumé was filled with great works, but he states in Philippians 3:9, *"And be found in him, not having mine own righteousness, which is of the law, but that which is through the faith of Christ, the righteousness which is of God by faith."*

As Christians, we understand clearly that salvation is through faith alone, yet why is it that we have such difficulty *living by faith*? The Lord undoubtedly saw this deficiency in our lives when He ponders in Luke 18:8: *"...Nevertheless when the Son of man cometh, shall he find faith on the earth?"* The Christian life is a daily walk of faith: *"For we walk by faith, not by sight"* (2 Corinthians 5:7). Paul states it very bluntly in Romans 14:23, *"And he that doubteth is damned if he eat, because he eateth not of faith: for whatsoever is not of faith is sin."*

What in your life today is not of faith? Is your salvation by faith? Is your separation by faith? Is your sanctification by faith? Is your stewardship by faith? Is your service by faith? If it isn't—it is impossible to please God with your life!

You have an obligation of faith.

## B. The Object of Faith

To some degree, every human being exercises faith. Many people have faith in themselves. Others place their faith in other people, or the government, or their jobs. Perhaps the people of Nineveh were similarly trusting something up until this time, but here in verse five of chapter three, it says they believed *God*!

Where is your faith? Acts 4:12 says, *"Neither is there salvation in any other: for there is none other name under heaven given among men, whereby we must be saved"* (Acts 4:12). The church, a preacher or priest, your good works, nor your money can save you—your only hope is Jesus Christ who said, *"I am the way, the truth, and the life: no man cometh unto the Father, but by me"* (John 14:6).

The believer must also remind himself daily, that he cannot live the Christian life without a constant reliance on faith in God. *"I am the vine, ye are the branches: He that abideth in me, and I in him, the same bringeth forth*

*much fruit: for without me ye can do nothing*" (John 15:5).
"*Except the LORD build the house, they labour in vain that build it: except the LORD keep the city, the watchman waketh but in vain*" (Psalm 127:1).

While our human nature wants to proudly claim our own achievements, we are not "*…sufficient of ourselves to think any thing as of ourselves; but our sufficiency is of God*" (2 Corinthians 3:5).

## II.  A Fast

"*…and proclaimed a fast, and put on sackcloth, from the greatest of them even to the least of them…And he caused it to be proclaimed and published through Nineveh by the decree of the king and his nobles, saying, Let neither man nor beast, herd nor flock, taste any thing: let them not feed, nor drink water.*"—JONAH 3:5, 7

### A.  *The Ultimate Contrition*

When a person denies himself of his most basic necessity—food—it shows a serious level of contrition. Fasting in the Old Testament was usually done in a very desperate situation when God's judgment was about to fall. King Ahab was a wicked man who deserved God's wrath, but in 1 Kings 21:27 we read, "*And it came to pass, when Ahab heard those words, that he rent his clothes, and put sackcloth upon his flesh, and fasted, and lay in sackcloth, and went softly.*"

The psalmist said, "*…I humbled my soul with fasting*" (Psalm 35:13). In Psalm 69:10, we read, "*When I wept, and chastened my soul with fasting….*" When repentance is accompanied by a sorrowful self-denial, God's attention is arrested, for: *"The sacrifices of God are a broken spirit: a broken and a contrite heart, O God, thou wilt not despise"* (Psalm 51:17).

## B. A Universal Commitment

Amazingly in this passage, it is not only the king and the people who fast, but even the animals were denied food and water! *"Let neither man nor beast, herd nor flock, taste any thing: let them not feed, nor drink water: But let man and beast be covered with sackcloth, and cry mightily unto God…"* (Jonah 3:7–8).

Having been raised on a farm, when animals are not fed and watered, they can make some noise! What a horrible sound this must have been as man and beast cried *"mightily unto God."*

While God can hear and answer the prayer of one individual, there is a unique power when there is a corporate humility before God. We are all familiar with the preaching of Peter on the day of Pentecost and the miraculous conversion and baptism of three thousand souls! But back up to chapter one in the book of Acts, and notice in verse fourteen it says, *"These **all** continued with one accord in prayer and supplication, with the women, and Mary the mother of Jesus, and with his brethren."* Chapter two opens in verse one by telling us, *"And when the day of Pentecost was fully come, they were all with one accord in one place."*

Universal commitment results in unbelievable changes!

# III. A Forsaking

Biblical repentance involves more than agreeing with God about our sin. Proverbs 28:13 reminds us that *"forsaking"* along with confession is necessary for mercy. Paul emphasizes this forsaking in Ephesians 4:22: *"That ye put off concerning the former conversation the old man, which is corrupt according to the deceitful lusts."*

*"Let the wicked forsake his way, and the unrighteous man his thoughts: and let him return unto the LORD, and he will have mercy upon him; and to our God, for he will abundantly pardon."*—ISAIAH 55:7

Here in Jonah chapter three, the people are instructed to have faith, to fast, and now to forsake their sin in verse eight: *"…yea, let them turn every one from his evil way, and from the violence that is in their hands."*

## A. *Repentance Involves a Change of Direction*

The word *repentance* literally means "to change direction," or "an about face." *"Therefore say unto the house of Israel, Thus saith the Lord GOD; Repent, and turn yourselves from your idols; and turn away your faces from all your abominations"* (Ezekiel 14:6).

The people here in Jonah 3:8 were challenged to turn from their evil *way*. They were going the wrong way and needed to change direction.

## B. *Repentance Involves a Change of Deeds*

Not only does verse eight reveal that the people were to change direction or their "way," but they were also to turn from the violence that was in their hands.

Everybody in their right mind wants to change their direction from Hell to Heaven and from God's judgment to God's blessing, but not everyone is willing to change their lifestyle.

*"And this is the condemnation, that light is come into the world, and men loved darkness rather than light, because their deeds were evil. For every one that doeth evil hateth the light, neither cometh to the light, lest his deeds should be reproved. But he that doeth truth cometh to the light, that his deeds may be made manifest, that they are wrought in God."*—JOHN 3:19–21

Many people today want the blessings of God while hanging on to the benefits of the world. God says, *"Love not the world, neither the things that are in the world. If any man love the world, the love of the Father is not in him. For all that is in the world, the lust of the flesh, and the lust of the eyes, and the pride of life, is not of the Father, but is of the world. And the world passeth away, and the lust thereof: but he that doeth the will of God abideth for ever"* (1 John 2:15–17).

True repentance means that *"...old things are passed away; behold, all things are become new"* (2 Corinthians 5:17).

## IV. A Forgiveness

*"Who can tell if God will turn and repent, and turn away from his fierce anger, that we perish not? And God saw their works, that they turned from their evil way; and God repented of the evil, that he had said that he would do unto them; and he did it not."*—JONAH 3:9–10

We cannot demand that God do any thing. We see this truth in Acts 8:22: *"Repent therefore of this thy wickedness, and pray God, if perhaps the thought of thine heart may be forgiven thee…."* However, when God sees true repentance and faith—there is forgiveness!

*"But there is forgiveness with thee"* (Psalm 130:4). *"If we confess our sins, he is faithful and just to forgive us our sins, and to cleanse us from all unrighteousness"* (1 John 1:9).

## A. The Attention of God

*"And God saw their works…"* (Jonah 3:10). God is not influenced by the outward appearance or by the impression of others. He Himself is able to read the heart of man. *"And needed not that any should testify of man: for he knew what was in man"* (John 2:25). *"I the LORD search the heart, I try the reins, even to give every man according to his ways, and according to the fruit of his doings"* (Jeremiah 17:10).

God's attention is drawn to the person who is repentant: *"…but to this man will I look, even to him that is poor and of a contrite spirit, and trembleth at my word"* (Isaiah 66:2). *"Though the LORD be high, yet hath he respect unto the lowly: but the proud he knoweth afar off"* (Psalm 138:6).

If you want God's attention, make sure you put on a humble spirit daily, *"for God resisteth the proud, and giveth grace to the humble"* (1 Peter 5:5).

## B. The Atonement of God

*"…and God repented of the evil, that he had said that he would do unto them; and he did it not"* (Jonah 3:10). We may not understand why God forgave these people of

Nineveh (Jonah didn't), *"But the mercy of the LORD is from everlasting to everlasting upon them that fear him, and his righteousness unto children's children"* (Psalm 103:17). Joel 2:13 sums up well what happened here to these people in Nineveh. *"And rend your heart, and not your garments, and turn unto the LORD your God: for he is gracious and merciful, slow to anger, and of great kindness, and repenteth him of the evil."*

We ought to be thankful for the grace of God every day of our lives. *"It is of the LORD's mercies that we are not consumed, because his compassions fail not. They are new every morning…"* (Lamentations 3:22–23).

Don't be afraid to go to God. Perhaps you have been away from the Lord for a long time—*"…he ever liveth to make intercession for them"* (Hebrews 7:25).

> Just as I am, without one plea,
> But that Thy blood was shed for me.
> And that Thou biddest me, come to Thee,
> O Lamb of God, I come.
>
> Just as I am, and waiting not,
> To rid my soul of one dark blot.
> To Thee whose blood can cleanse each spot,
> O Lamb of God, I come.
>
> Just as I am, Thou wilt receive,
> Wilt welcome, pardon, cleanse, relieve.
> Because Thy promise, I believe,
> O Lamb of God, I come.

SECTION THREE

# A Strange Conclusion

# A Pouting Prophet

## Key Verses

*"But it displeased Jonah exceedingly, and he was very angry. And he prayed unto the LORD, and said, I pray thee, O LORD, was not this my saying, when I was yet in my country? Therefore I fled before unto Tarshish: for I knew that thou art a gracious God, and merciful, slow to anger, and of great kindness, and repentest thee of the evil."*—JONAH 4:1–2

## Overview

Often the greatest tests will come in our lives after the greatest victories. Right after the Lord's baptism and the words from Heaven, "…*This is my beloved Son, in whom I am well pleased*," Jesus faced the temptation of the devil in the desert. No sooner had Elijah called down fire from Heaven, he is seen running for his life from Jezebel! Satan never rests. While we may experience victory today, we can be sure he is planning an attack for tomorrow.

## Lesson Theme

Satan is always trying to steal attention away from God. This is often accomplished in our lives when he gets us to focus on ourselves. Jonah was more concerned about being "right" than he was about "revival." Would we be thankful for a revival that *didn't* involve us? We must guard against the *"spirit that dwelleth in us lusteth to envy"* (James 4:5).

# Lesson Objectives

- To help the student understand that Satan never gives up in his attempts to make us ineffective.
- To teach the student that Satan's most vicious attacks in our lives will come after some of God's greatest victories.
- To show the student the effects of three very deadly sins: selfishness, anger, and slander.
- To help the student to understand that we must never blame God for our circumstances.

# Teaching Outline

I. A Selfish Displeasure
   - A.  Selfishness Is a Killer of Joy
   - B.  Selfishness Is a Kindred to Jealousy

II. A Surly Disposition
   - A.  The Demeanor of Anger
   - B.  The Disgrace of Anger
   - C.  The Damage of Anger

III. A Slanderous Defense
   - A.  An Inaccurate Exposé
   - B.  An Insulting Excuse

# A Pouting Prophet

## Text

*"But it displeased Jonah exceedingly, and he was very angry. And he prayed unto the LORD, and said, I pray thee, O LORD, was not this my saying, when I was yet in my country? Therefore I fled before unto Tarshish: for I knew that thou art a gracious God, and merciful, slow to anger, and of great kindness, and repentest thee of the evil."*—JONAH 4:1–2

An entire city has just been converted through one sermon! If this isn't the greatest revival on record it certainly is one of the quickest! It took longer for God to get the preacher to be willing to go preach than it did for God to change the city. Jonah witnessed something that very few people will ever witness—genuine revival. In fact, the only person who didn't have revival was the evangelist!

# I. A Selfish Displeasure

In 2 Timothy 3:1, the Bible says, *"This know also, that in the last days perilous times shall come."* What are the characteristics of these perilous last days? No doubt crime, political corruption, moral indecencies, and religious hypocrisy, right? No. Verse two tells us the problem of the peril: *"For men shall be lovers of their own selves...."*

D.L. Moody used to say, "The man I fear the most is the one who walks underneath this hat." When Abraham Lincoln was running for President of the United States, a reporter asked him if he feared any of his opponents. He said, "Yes, one." The reporter was somewhat surprised and said, "Which one?" Lincoln responded by saying, "A man named Lincoln. If I am defeated, I will be defeated by a man named Lincoln."

Every single person in Jonah chapter three experienced revival except Jonah. He was his own worst enemy! Why?

## A. Selfishness Is a Killer of Joy

Pity parties are not happy events! No one is ever happy sitting in a corner feeling sorry for himself. Paul reminds us that selfishness kills joy every single time in our lives. *"Fulfil ye my joy, that ye be likeminded, having the same love, being of one accord, of one mind. Let nothing be done through strife or vainglory; but in lowliness of mind let each esteem other better than themselves. Look not every man on his own things, but every man also on the things of others"* (Philippians 2:2–4).

Too often, we serve God, or perhaps do what is right, because of what is in it for ourselves. Paul shows us just the opposite motivation in 1 Corinthians 10:33: *"Even as*

*I please all men in all things, not seeking mine own profit, but the profit of many, that they may be saved."*

Whether it is in ministry, or in your family, or in society—remember, love *"...seeketh not her own"* (1 Corinthians 13:5).

## B. Selfishness Is a Kindred to Jealousy

It is easy to see the jealousy that is present here in Jonah's life. He was sure that Nineveh deserved judgment, just as he had received for his disobedience. He wants them to have to do a little "whale" time as well.

It didn't fare very well for Joseph's brothers when they became jealous of his "coat of many colors." Nothing but trouble followed them the rest of their lives.

*"And when his brethren saw that their father loved him more than all his brethren, they hated him, and could not speak peaceably unto him."*—GENESIS 37:4

Saul's demise started when he heard the women singing and praising David for killing Goliath. *"And Saul was very wroth, and the saying displeased him; and he said, They have ascribed unto David ten thousands, and to me they have ascribed but thousands: and what can he have more but the kingdom?"* (1 Samuel 18:8).

The elder son in Luke 15 didn't care about the disobedience of his brother until he repented and came home. *"And he was angry, and would not go in..."* (Luke 15:28).

Proverbs 6:34 warns us, *"For jealousy is the rage of a man...."*

## II. A Surly Disposition

*"…and he was very angry."*—JONAH 4:1

Anger is one letter short of danger! It is interesting to note that in the passages cited earlier about Joseph's brothers, King Saul, and the elder son—anger is mentioned in connection with their jealous and selfish dispositions. Someone once said, "I get angry, but it's all over in a minute." Well, so is the nuclear bomb!

### A. The Demeanor of Anger

Have you ever met people who just seemed to have a chip on their shoulders? It seems that no matter what happens to them, they are always angry about something. Anger has become a life-dominating problem. Hebrews 12:15 informs us to be on guard against a *"root of bitterness."* This root *"springing up"* will *"trouble you"* and as a result, many will *"be defiled."*

Do you find yourself angry when others are rejoicing? Check your roots! There is a cause to this demeanor of anger.

Be sure to notice what God says and what He calls the angry person in Ecclesiastes 7:9, *"Be not hasty in thy spirit to be angry: for anger resteth in the bosom of fools."*

### B. The Disgrace of Anger

What an absolute disgrace it is that in the midst of this wonderful revival in Nineveh, Jonah is sulking and seething in anger! Proverbs 14:17 tells us, *"He that is soon angry dealeth foolishly: and a man of wicked devices is hated."* An angry person is never a respected person. No one wants to follow someone who is angry.

Matthew 5:22 warns us of the results of anger: *"But I say unto you, That whosoever is angry with his brother without a cause shall be in danger of the judgment...."*

## C. The Damage of Anger

Someone has wisely stated, "Anger is like acid. It does more damage to the container in which it is stored than on anything that it is poured." We think that we are punishing others by being angry when in truth, we are destroying ourselves!

There was once a Quaker who owned a very ornery cow. Every time he milked her, it was a clash of two wills. This particular morning she was unusually irritable, but he was determined to endure the session without speaking so much as a cross word. As the farmer began to milk her, ol' Bossy stepped on his foot with all her weight. He struggled silently, groaned a little under his breath, pulled his foot free, then sat back down on the stool. She then swished her tail in his face like a long string whip. He merely leaned away so it wouldn't be able to reach him. Next she kicked over the bucket, by then half-full of warm milk. He started over, mumbling a few words to himself, but he never lost his cool. Once finished with the ordeal, he breathed a sigh of relief, picked up the bucket and stool, and as he was leaving she hauled off and kicked him against the barn wall twelve feet away. That did it! He stood to his feet, marched in front of his cow, stared into those big eyes, and as he shook a long bony finger in her face, he shouted, "Thou dost know that I am a Quaker. Thou dost know also that I cannot strike thee back...but I can sell thee to a Presbyterian!"

Get a handle on your anger! First Corinthians 9:25 says, *"And every man that striveth for the mastery is temperate in all things…."* By the grace of God we must be self-disciplined in our spirits.

*"He that is slow to anger is better than the mighty; and he that ruleth his spirit than he that taketh a city."*
—PROVERBS 16:32

Not only do our actions get us in trouble in life, but our reactions do, as well. We need to exercise discretion with respect to those reactions. Proverbs 19:11 states, *"The discretion of a man deferreth his anger; and it is his glory to pass over a transgression."* God gives great advice in James 1:19, *"Wherefore, my beloved brethren, let every man be swift to hear, slow to speak, slow to wrath."*

# III.  A Slanderous Defense

*"And he prayed unto the LORD, and said, I pray thee, O LORD, was not this my saying, when I was yet in my country? Therefore I fled before unto Tarshish: for I knew that thou art a gracious God, and merciful, slow to anger, and of great kindness, and repentest thee of the evil."*—JONAH 4:2

## A.  An Inaccurate Exposé

This is about as low as a man can sink! Jonah is accusing God of being wrong. Selfishness and surliness will lead you to slander. These character flaws will cause you to think if you can't be right, then nobody's going to be right—not even God!

We can never question God's ways. He doesn't have to explain Himself. Perhaps we would have chosen to destroy the people of Nineveh, but we do not possess the grace and mercy that our God does.

*"For my thoughts are not your thoughts, neither are your ways my ways, saith the LORD. For as the heavens are higher than the earth, so are my ways higher than your ways, and my thoughts than your thoughts."*—ISAIAH 55:8–9

*"As for God, his way is perfect..."* (Psalm 18:30). We may not always understand, but, *"The LORD is righteous in all his ways, and holy in all his works"* (Psalm 145:17).

Be careful of your thoughts toward God. As clay we must not question the Potter. *"Therefore hath he mercy on whom he will have mercy, and whom he will he hardeneth. Thou wilt say then unto me, Why doth he yet find fault? For who hath resisteth his will? Nay but, O man, who art thou that repliest against God? Shall the thing formed say to him that formed it, Why hast thou made me thus? Hath not the potter power over the clay, of the same lump to make one vessel unto honour, and another unto dishonour?"* (Romans 9:18–21).

## B. An Insulting Excuse

Even more disgusting than Jonah's accusation against God's mercy is his sorry excuse for his own disobedience. He has the gall in verse two to tell God that it was this very mercy of God that caused him to disobey in the first place! *"Therefore I fled before unto Tarshish: for I knew that thou art a gracious God, and merciful, slow to anger, and of great kindness, and repentest thee of the evil."*

It is a dangerous thing to slander the Lord. Proverbs 19:3 states, *"The foolishness of man perverteth his way: and his heart fretteth against the LORD."* Paul warns us in Philippians 2:14, *"Do all things without murmurings and disputings."*

Are you murmuring in your life today against God for something that did not go well in your past? Are you disputing with Him about how you have been treated or about your "lot in life"? The Corinthian church fell into that mode, and Paul gave them a little history lesson from the children of Israel and sternly stated, *"Neither murmur ye, as some of them also murmured, and were destroyed of the destroyer"* (1 Corinthians 10:10).

The next time you think you got a raw deal—think about Jesus on the Cross. Did He deserve to be spit upon, cursed and crucified? He was without sin. Pilate found no fault in Him.

*"Who did no sin, neither was guile found in his mouth: Who, when he was reviled, reviled not again; when he suffered, he threatened not; but committed himself to him that judgeth righteously."*—1 PETER 2:22–23

# A Pathetic Position

## Key Verse

*"Therefore now, O Lord, take, I beseech thee, my life from me; for it is better for me to die than to live."*—Jonah 4:3

## Overview

Disobedience, selfishness, anger, and bitterness can be kept inside for awhile, but eventually *"as he thinketh in his heart, so is he"* (Proverbs 23:7). God admonishes us to *"Keep thy heart with all diligence; for out of it are the issues of life"* (Proverbs 4:23).

The real Jonah is about to stand up!

## Lesson Theme

Jonah is perhaps for the first time truly being honest with God. What is down in his heart is coming to the surface, and it's not a pleasant revelation. We must learn to be honest about our true condition before God, because the longer we live in phoniness or hypocrisy, the more miserable we will be in the end.

## Lesson Objectives

- To help the student understand that we are not merely human beings but human "becomings" and everything we do today has an impact on what we will become in the future.

- To strengthen the student's conviction about the origin and sanctity of life.
- To challenge the student to live his life for that which is eternal rather than for that which is temporal.
- To enable the student to see how valuable his life can be if yielded completely to God's perfect will.

## Teaching Outline

I. A Pitiful Prayer
   A. A Childish Paradigm
   B. A Careless Proposition
   C. A Candid Presumption

II. A Perverted Pondering
   A. The Schedule of Life Is Unknown
   B. The Sacredness of Life Is Unmistakable
   C. The Stewardship of Life Is Unconditional
   D. The Significance of Life Is Unbelievable

# A Pathetic Position

## Text

*"Therefore now, O L*ORD*, take, I beseech thee, my life from me; for it is better for me to die than to live."*—J*ONAH* 4:3

Listen to this prayer of Jonah in chapter four and verse three, *"Therefore now, O L*ORD*, take, I beseech thee, my life from me; for it is better for me to die than to live."* One word comes to my mind—PATHETIC! Suicide is a terrible sin against oneself and is surely bad enough, but when a man asks God to kill him—that's pretty low! If God didn't want us to live He wouldn't have created us in the first place. If our lives are no longer useful here on earth, He can take us to Heaven. To presume that we know better than God about our lives, is a pathetic position.

# I.  A Pitiful Prayer

If we are not careful, prayer can become very selfish. We can spend our whole time with the Lord griping about how tough life has become and handing Him a list of things that He needs to change as soon as possible. We fail to take time to thank Him for our blessings, adore His name, and just spend quality time meditating on Him. When our prayers become self-centered, we are like the Pharisee who, *"stood and prayed thus with **himself…**"* (Luke 18:11). Those prayers never reach God—they only give a false sense of satisfaction.

## A.  A Childish Paradigm

We've seen Jonah's selfishness all the way through this book, but his childish perspective really stands out here. Children have a very limited and introverted paradigm. They don't see the danger of playing with matches or running in the street. Often when they do not get their way they throw temper tantrums. Jonah is acting very much like a little child here. He hasn't gotten *his* way, so now he doesn't want *any* way.

When life ends, will it really matter where we lived, or how much money we made, or how much fun we had or didn't have? Someone has said that "life is our opportunity to prepare to meet God." That's really all life is! When life ends, all that will matter is that we are able to *"…stand perfect and complete in all the will of God"* (Colossians 4:12).

## B.  A Careless Proposition

When we are upset or discouraged, we can say some really stupid things that we regret later. Now to be sure,

Jonah does not completely understand why God has been merciful to Nineveh, but is a lack of understanding reason to hate your life?

First John 5:3 tells us, *"For this is the love of God, that we keep his commandments: and his commandments are not grievous."* God doesn't intend that any part of His will for our lives be a burden. In fact, Jesus said, *"...I am come that they might have life, and that they might have it more abundantly"* (John 10:10). God promises, *"They shall be abundantly satisfied with the fatness of thy house; and thou shalt make them drink of the river of thy pleasures"* (Psalm 36:8).

Even when life takes its negative turns, God promises, *"...My grace is sufficient for thee: for my strength is made perfect in weakness."* So great was this grace that Paul could proclaim: *"Most gladly therefore will I rather glory in my infirmities, that the power of Christ may rest upon me. Therefore I take pleasure in infirmities, in reproaches, in necessities, in persecutions, in distresses for Christ's sake: for when I am weak, then am I strong"* (2 Corinthians 12:9–10).

## C. A Candid Presumption

Who are we to presume that our lives are no longer useful or needed? First Samuel 2:6 reminds us, *"The LORD killeth, and maketh alive: he bringeth down to the grave, and bringeth up."* Paul pointed the people to the living God in his sermon on Mars' Hill when he said, *"God that made the world and all things therein, seeing that he is Lord of heaven and earth, dwelleth not in temples made with hands; Neither is worshipped with men's hands, as though he needed any thing, seeing he giveth to all life, and breath, and all things.... For in him we live, and move, and have our being..."* (Acts 17:24–25,28).

Regardless of our circumstances, we should endeavor to make every day that God gives us count for Him. *"So teach us to number our days, that we may apply our hearts unto wisdom"* (Psalm 90:12).

*"Redeeming the time, because the days are evil."*
—EPHESIANS 5:16

## II. A Perverted Pondering

Meditation seems to be a lost art. We seem to be too busy to ponder the blessings of God and His will for our lives. But meditation can also be very dangerous if not disciplined toward that which is proper. The prophet Jeremiah sternly reminds us, *"The heart is deceitful above all things, and desperately wicked: who can know it?"* (Jeremiah 17:9).

Jonah's heart was in no condition to be meditating! Since his initial disobedience, the momentum in his life was negative. It is no great wonder then, that his conclusion about his life was also negative.

Listen to what Paul instructs us with respect to a disciplined meditation, *"Be careful for nothing; but in every thing by prayer and supplication with thanksgiving let your requests be made known unto God. And the peace of God, which passeth all understanding, shall keep your hearts and minds through Christ Jesus. Finally, brethren, whatsoever things are true, whatsoever things are honest, whatsoever things are just, whatsoever things are pure, whatsoever things are lovely, whatsoever things are of good report; if there be any virtue, and if there be any praise, think on these things. Those things, which ye have both learned, and received, and heard, and seen in me, do: and the God of peace shall be with you"* (Philippians 4:6–9).

Jonah had become so negative about life that his thoughts were only on death. What a tragedy when man loses his love for life as God intended!

## A. The Schedule of Life Is Unknown

Most of us would love to live a long and full life. But life itself teaches us that there are no guarantees.

*"Boast not thyself of to morrow; for thou knowest not what a day may bring forth."*—PROVERBS 27:1

*"…For what is your life? It is even a vapour, that appeareth for a little time, and then vanisheth away."* —JAMES 4:14

A person does not die because he gets old, or sick, or suffers some unfortunate accident. The Bible tells us in Hebrews 9:27 that *"…it is appointed unto men once to die…."* Notice, it is appointed! Solomon of old said, *"A time to be born, and a time to die…"* (Ecclesiastes 3:2). Each of us has a birthday. We know when we were born and have birth certificates to prove it. Each of us, according to the Bible, has a death day. We do not know when it is, but one day, there will be a death certificate to prove it.

## B. The Sacredness of Life Is Unmistakable

John 1:3–4 declares: *"All things were made by him; and without him was not any thing made that was made. In him was life…."* I love the detailed description by the psalmist in Psalm 139 as he informs us that life begins at conception, and God is there from the very first moment of existence.

*"For thou hast possessed my reins: thou hast covered me in my mother's womb. I will praise thee; for I am fearfully and wonderfully made: marvellous are thy works; and that my soul knoweth right well. My substance was not hid from thee, when I was made in secret, and curiously wrought in the lowest parts of the earth. Thine eyes did see my substance, yet being unperfect; and in thy book all my members were written, which in continuance were fashioned, when as yet there was none of them. How precious also are thy thoughts unto me, O God! how great is the sum of them!"* (Psalm 139:13–17).

God puts a huge value on life and depends on us to protect its sanctity. *"Whoso sheddeth man's blood, by man shall his blood be shed: for in the image of God made he man"* (Genesis 9:6).

The world today puts so little value on life. The poor, the homeless, the unborn child, the elderly, or misfortunate seem to be just a matter of statistics. Death, it seems, is just another brutal fact of life. One day, God will show us just how valuable life is to Him when He *"… shall wipe away all tears from their eyes; and there shall be no more death…"* (Revelation 21:4). Yes, God victoriously announces in 1 Corinthians 15:26, *"The last enemy that shall be destroyed is death."*

### C. The Stewardship of Life Is Unconditional

God created us for one reason: to glorify Him.

*"That we should be to the praise of his glory…"* (Ephesians 1:12). *"Thou art worthy, O Lord, to receive glory and honour and power: for thou hast created all things, and for thy pleasure they are and were created"* (Revelation 4:11).

The life of the Christian is no longer his—it belongs to God! *"What? know ye not that your body is the temple of the Holy Ghost which is in you, which ye have of God, and ye are not your own? For ye are bought with a price: therefore glorify God in your body, and in your spirit, which are God's"* (1 Corinthians 6:19–20). Paul admonishes God's people in 2 Corinthians 5:15, *"And that he died for all, that they which live should not henceforth live unto themselves, but unto him which died for them, and rose again."*

Our lot in life has nothing to do with how we use our lives. Rich or poor, healthy or well, married or unmarried, welcomed or forsaken, appreciated or despised—we must all steward our lives wisely.

*"…so now also Christ shall be magnified in my body, whether it be by life, or by death. For to me to live is Christ, and to die is gain."*—PHILIPPIANS 1:20–21

None of us have an excuse to end life or live it for anything or any one other than the One Who gave it to us. *"Whether therefore ye eat, or drink, or whatsoever ye do, do all to the glory of God"* (1 Corinthians 10:31).

### D. The Significance of Life Is Unbelievable

I have often wondered if God had any more cities that needed a sermon from Jonah. Perhaps God wanted this revival in Nineveh to spread across an entire continent like the days of the Great Awakening. But we'll never know, because this pouting prophet couldn't see past himself!

Sure, life takes its negative turns and seems harsh at times, but it is never insignificant. Fanny Crosby, the blind hymn-writer said, "I don't believe I would have ever written all of those hymns had I been able to see."

God has a reason for everything that has come your way in life and if you will let Him, He'll show you that *"...all things work together for good to them that love God, to them who are the called according to his purpose"* (Romans 8:28).

God used an insignificant rod in Exodus 4:2; an insignificant jaw bone in Judges 15:15; five insignificant smooth stones in 1 Samuel 17:40; an insignificant amount of meal and oil in 1 Kings 17:12; an insignificant cloud the size of a man's hand in 1 Kings 18:44; the insignificant mustard seed in Matthew 13:32; five insignificant loaves and two small fishes in John 6:9—but all were necessary for God to do great miracles!

No doubt that is why God asks in Zechariah 4:10, *"For who hath despised the day of small things?...."* For it is these *"weak," "foolish," "base,"* and *"despised"* things that God has chosen *"...to bring to nought things that are"* (1 Corinthians 1:27–28).

> Give then the best you have, not for reward:
> Not for the praise of men, but for the Lord.
>
> Every work for Jesus will be blest,
> For He asks from every one his best
>
> Our talents may be few—these may be small,
> But unto Him is due our best, our all!

LESSON THIRTEEN

# A Painful Prison

## Key Verses

*"Then said the L‍ord, Doest thou well to be angry? So Jonah went out of the city, and sat on the east side of the city, and there made him a booth, and sat under it in the shadow, till he might see what would become of the city. And the L‍ord God prepared a gourd, and made it to come up over Jonah, that it might be a shadow over his head, to deliver him from his grief. So Jonah was exceeding glad of the gourd. But God prepared a worm when the morning rose the next day, and it smote the gourd that it withered. And it came to pass, when the sun did arise, that God prepared a vehement east wind; and the sun beat upon the head of Jonah, that he fainted, and wished in himself to die, and said, It is better for me to die than to live. And God said to Jonah, Doest thou well to be angry for the gourd? And he said, I do well to be angry, even unto death. Then said the L‍ord, Thou hast had pity on the gourd, for the which thou hast not laboured, neither madest it grow; which came up in a night, and perished in a night: And should not I spare Nineveh, that great city, wherein are more than sixscore thousand persons that cannot discern between their right hand and their left hand; and also much cattle?"*—J‍onah 4:4–11

## Overview

This really is a sad and strange conclusion to what should have been a joyful summary of one of the greatest revivals ever! The truth is, Satan never stops working. Sometimes in the midst of the greatest miracles, we experience tragedy and defeat because we take our focus off of God and place it on ourselves.

## Lesson Theme

It has been said, "At the heart of the problem is a problem of the heart." Also, "When the heart is not pure—the vision is unclear." While Jonah delivered God's message to the people of Nineveh, he never allowed God's message to reach his own heart. *"For from within, out of the heart of men, proceed evil thoughts, adulteries, fornications, murders, Thefts, covetousness, wickedness, deceit, lasciviousness, an evil eye, blasphemy, pride, foolishness: All these evil things come from within, and defile the man"* (Mark 7:21–23).

## Lesson Objectives

- To establish the fact that the student's spirit or attitude in life is the determining factor for his view of life.
- To give an understanding to the student that we are our own worst enemies when we fail to submit to God's plan for our lives.
- To reinforce the message that selfishness is never the way to happiness, but rather to frustration and defeat.
- To develop in the life of the student a gratefulness that will be pleasing to God and to those around us.

## Teaching Outline

I. A Contentious Intolerance
   A. An Incorrigible Attitude
   B. An Incarcerating Attitude

II. A Continuous Independence
   A. A Lack of Joy

    B.   A Lingering of Jealousy
    C.   A Looking for Judgment

III.  A Covetous Ingratitude
    A.   A Misunderstood Condolence
    B.   A Missing Characteristic
    C.   A Merciful Climax

# A Painful Prison

## Text

*"Then said the LORD, Doest thou well to be angry? So Jonah went out of the city, and sat on the east side of the city, and there made him a booth, and sat under it in the shadow, till he might see what would become of the city. And the LORD God prepared a gourd, and made it to come up over Jonah, that it might be a shadow over his head, to deliver him from his grief. So Jonah was exceeding glad of the gourd. But God prepared a worm when the morning rose the next day, and it smote the gourd that it withered. And it came to pass, when the sun did arise, that God prepared a vehement east wind; and the sun beat upon the head of Jonah, that he fainted, and wished in himself to die, and said, It is better for me to die than to live. And God said to Jonah, Doest thou well to be angry for the gourd? And he said, I do well to be angry, even unto death. Then said the LORD, Thou hast had pity on the gourd, for the which thou hast not laboured, neither madest it grow; which*

*came up in a night, and perished in a night: And should not I spare Nineveh, that great city, wherein are more than sixscore thousand persons that cannot discern between their right hand and their left hand; and also much cattle?"*—JONAH 4:4–11

No doubt you have heard the expression, "You made your bed—now you have to sleep in it!" That is basically the dilemma that Jonah faces here as this book closes. Everything has changed around him, but Jonah's heart remains unchanged! He is probably more miserable now than he was in the belly of the whale. (At least he wasn't asking to die back then!) I'm afraid there are a lot of people today spending their lives in prisons without bars.

# I.   A Contentious Intolerance

*"Then said the LORD, Doest thou well to be angry?…And he said, I do well to be angry, even unto death."*—Jonah 4:4,9

## A.  An Incorrigible Attitude

God has been merciful and gracious, slow to anger, and plenteous in mercy, but Jonah remains sullen and disgusted in spirit.

Proverbs 20:27 says, *"The spirit of man is the candle of the LORD, searching all the inward parts of the belly."* It is often said that "attitude determines altitude." At this point in the story, Jonah is of no value to the work of God because of his lousy attitude.

The most dangerous thing about an evil spirit is that it is contagious. I believe that is why God tried to console Jonah here and pull him out of the depths of his despair. Jonah was a danger to every one around him. Proverbs

29:8 says, *"Scornful men bring a city into a snare...."* James warns us of the danger of this type of person, *"But if ye have bitter envying and strife in your hearts, glory not, and lie not against the truth. This wisdom descendeth not from above, but is earthly, sensual, devilish. For where envying and strife is, there is confusion and every evil work"* (James 3:14–16).

Listen to the concern in Paul's voice as he speaks to the Christians at Rome, *"Now I beseech you, brethren, mark them which cause divisions and offences contrary to the doctrine which ye have learned; and avoid them. For they that are such serve not our Lord Jesus Christ, but their own belly; and by good words and fair speeches deceive the hearts of the simple"* (Romans 16:17–18).

## B. An Incarcerating Attitude

*"Jesus answered them, Verily, verily, I say unto you, Whosoever committeth sin is the servant of sin"* (John 8:34).

Jonah built the bars that held him in his sinful attitude. *"His own iniquities shall take the wicked himself, and he shall be holden with the cords of his sins"* (Proverbs 5:22). *"Know ye not, that to whom ye yield yourselves servants to obey; his servants ye are to whom ye obey; whether of sin unto death, or of obedience unto righteousness?"* (Romans 6:16).

You can play around with sin just like you can choose to have a baby python snake for a pet. But just like that snake, the problem with a little sin is that it never stays little. One day, when that python of sin wraps itself around your life, you will have no power to free yourself from its grip.

Jonah—*"For I perceive that thou art in the gall of bitterness, and in the bond of iniquity"* (Acts 8:23).

# II. A Continuous Independence

*"So Jonah went out of the city, and sat on the east side of the city, and there made him a booth, and sat under it in the shadow, till he might see what would become of the city."*—JONAH 4:5

The selfish disobedience that is easily seen in chapter one continues to the end of the story. While there were some desperate "foxhole" prayers in times of difficulty, nothing has really changed in Jonah's heart. He is still "doing that which is right in his own eyes."

## A. A Lack of Joy

Revival always brings joy.

> *"Then Philip went down to the city of Samaria, and preached Christ unto them. And the people with one accord gave heed unto those things which Philip spake, hearing and seeing the miracles which he did. For unclean spirits, crying with loud voice, came out of many that were possessed with them: and many taken with palsies, and that were lame, were healed. And there was great joy in that city."*—ACTS 8:5–8

No doubt there was a similar spirit here in the city of Nineveh following their repentance and faith. But while the burden of sin had been lifted from the hearts of countless thousands, Jonah sat along the side of the road on the east side of the city waiting and hoping for judgment to fall.

Jonah had a head-knowledge of what was right, but he had no heart to do what he knew. Joy in the Christian life does not come because of what we know. *"Knowledge puffeth up"* (1 Corinthians 8:1). Joy is a result of what we do with those things that we know to be true. *"If ye know these things, happy are ye if ye do them"* (John 13:17). *"But be ye doers of the word, and not hearers only, deceiving your own selves. For if any be a hearer of the word, and not a doer, he is like unto a man beholding his natural face in a glass: For he beholdeth himself, and goeth his way, and straightway forgetteth what manner of man he was. But whoso looketh into the perfect law of liberty, and continueth therein, he being not a forgetful hearer, but a doer of the work, this man shall be blessed in his deed"* (James 1:22–25).

Lack of joy is always a result of a lack of obedience.

## B. A Lingering of Jealousy

Jonah is still upset that in his mind God hasn't treated him fairly. Why should he suffer these things while Nineveh gets off "scott-free" just because they repented?

*"For jealousy is the rage of a man: therefore he will not spare in the day of vengeance. He will not regard any ransom; neither will he rest content, though thou givest many gifts."*—PROVERBS 6:34–35

The wisdom of Solomon is well stated in Song of Solomon 8:6, *"...jealousy is cruel as the grave: the coals thereof are coals of fire, which hath a most vehement flame."*

## C. A Looking for Judgment

*"...and there made him a booth, and sat under it in the shadow, till he might see what would become of the city"* (Jonah 4:5). Jonah is still waiting for God's judgment to fall on Nineveh! He has experienced personally the mercy of God, but he can't bring himself to believe that God is going to spare this city.

When God's Word is obeyed, God has a biblical track-record of forgiveness. And when God forgives, there is no lingering cloud of judgment. *"As far as the east is from the west, so far hath he removed our transgressions from us"* (Psalm 103:12). *"I, even I, am he that blotteth out thy transgressions for mine own sake, and will not remember thy sins"* (Isaiah 43:25).

# III. A Covetous Ingratitude

*"And the LORD God prepared a gourd, and made it to come up over Jonah, that it might be a shadow over his head, to deliver him from his grief. So Jonah was exceeding glad of the gourd. But God prepared a worm when the morning rose the next day, and it smote the gourd that it withered. And it came to pass, when the sun did arise, that God prepared a vehement east wind; and the sun beat upon the head of Jonah, that he fainted, and wished in himself to die, and said, It is better for me to die than to live. And God said to Jonah, Doest thou well to be angry for the gourd? And he said, I do well to be angry, even unto death."*—JONAH 4:6–9

## A. A Misunderstood Condolence

The gourd was a picture of God's mercy on Nineveh. Unlike the people of Nineveh however, Jonah is glad for the gourd but does not recognize it as a gift from God. He was *glad* for the gourd, but he was not *grateful* for the gourd or for the God who had provided it.

Jonah apparently feels that God owes him something. In reality, God doesn't have to do anything for us. We don't deserve His grace, but He is more than glad to give it to those who are grateful for such a gift. *"…God resisteth the proud, and giveth grace to the humble. Humble yourselves therefore under the mighty hand of God, that he may exalt you in due time"* (1 Peter 5:5–6). *"Though the LORD be high, yet hath he respect unto the lowly: but the proud he knoweth afar off"* (Psalm 138:6).

## B.  A Missing Characteristic

Check the book of Jonah carefully and see if you can find a time when Jonah is ever thankful. He wasn't thankful for God's will in his life. He was certainly not thankful for the chastisement. He is not thankful for a second chance. He was not thankful for the revival in Nineveh. He was not thankful for God's provision from the heat in chapter four. If we don't have a gratitude attitude—we simply have an attitude!

Romans 1 lists some despicable sins in verses twenty-six through thirty-one. The people who commit these terrible sins are described in verse thirty-two as: *"Who knowing the judgment of God, that they which commit such things are worthy of death, not only do the same, but have pleasure in them that do them."* A very sad state of affairs—sin is committed and the consequences are laughed to scorn! But where does this all start? What is the cause of such a condition? Read carefully Romans 1:21, for it is here that we see the genesis of this reprobate lifestyle. *"Because that, when they knew God, they glorified him not as God, neither were thankful…."*

Do you know God? Is He God in your life? Or, like Jonah, are you being your own God? The next step after a disobedient spirit is an ungrateful spirit—and the rest, as they say, is history!

147

## C. A Merciful Climax

*"Then said the LORD, Thou hast had pity on the gourd, for the which thou hast not laboured, neither madest it grow; which came up in a night, and perished in a night: And should not I spare Nineveh, that great city, wherein are more than sixscore thousand persons that cannot discern between their right hand and their left hand; and also much cattle?"*—JONAH 4:10–11

God closes this story with a reminder of His mercy. Perhaps in our opinion (and certainly Jonah's), Nineveh didn't deserve God's mercy. But the truth is, neither do we! Titus 3:5 states, *"Not by works of righteousness which we have done, but according to his mercy he saved us, by the washing of regeneration, and renewing of the Holy Ghost."* Indeed, *"it is of the LORD's mercies that we are not consumed…"* (Lamentations 3:22). Yes, *"by the grace of God I am what I am…"* (1 Corinthians 15:10).

> Marvelous grace of our loving Lord,
> Grace that exceeds our sin and our guilt.
> Yonder on Calvary's mount outpoured,
> There where the blood of the Lamb was spilt.
>
> Grace, Grace, God's Grace
> Grace that will pardon and cleanse within.
> Grace, Grace, God's Grace
> Grace that is greater than all our sin.

For additional Christian
growth resources visit
**www.strivingtogether.com**